LEADERSHIP
GEMS

RIA STORY

ISBN: 1543034969
ISBN-13: 978-1543034967

WHAT READERS ARE SAYING ABOUT LEADERSHIP GEMS

"A very thought provoking, and easy to read collection of truths….Ria explains them in a way that they are easy to remember, thus making it easier for the reader to understand and practice great leadership." J. Johnson

"What an inspiration you are to all of us especially the women audience. Your book is a clear example & step by step guide on how to become an effective leader. It is so easy to read and simple yet meaningful which is the beauty of this book." K. Poonawala

"What a great read! Thank you for such an inspiring and heartfelt book. Keep up the excellent work!" A. Ramirez

"I wanted to thank you for your book Leadership Gems (for Women). Your insights are right on target and this will help me in my work!" S. Guerard

DEDICATION

This book is dedicated to those with the courage to discover their true potential.

Mark Twain said, "The two greatest days in your life are the day you are born and the day you discover why." My "why" is to share my story and inspire you to reach your potential, regardless of your past or present circumstances.

CONTENTS

INTRODUCTION

Regardless of whether you are a front line employee or the CEO of a multi-billion dollar organization, the principles in this book will help you become more successful, more influential, and a higher level leader.

All of us have some influence naturally, and some of us have more than others. We are all influencing someone at some level, even though we may not realize it. Leadership is influence. Therefore, we are all "leaders." The question is, what are we doing with our influence? And, how can we increase it?

Natural ability isn't enough to help you be successful as a leader. You must intentionally develop your skills by developing the characteristics covered in this book, so you can lead and influence others at home, at work, at church, or even as a volunteer.

Leadership is one of the most profoundly complex, and at the same time, incredibly simple concepts.

John C. Maxwell states it well, *"Leadership is influence."* Influence is simple and easy to understand. If you are influencing someone to do, say, or think something different, you are leading them.

But understanding why, how, when, and who you are influencing becomes very complex. "How do I increase my influence (leadership) with others?" is a question all of us should devote significant time, thought, and consideration to.

We all want, and at some level need, to be successful in life. Relating leadership to success is fairly simple.

However, leadership is also extremely complex – because it's increased primarily by developing your character. Developing your character will improve your ability to influence (lead) yourself initially and others secondarily.

Your character is the determining success factor in your life. Your character is the defining factor in how you will face life's challenges. Your response to success, failure, joy, pain, sickness, health, poverty, or wealth will all be based upon your character. Character is far more than your talent, natural gifts, skills, and abilities. Character is the foundation upon which you will build your legacy.

Character is based upon intangible characteristics that will determine your success: attitude, work ethic, perseverance, resilience, discipline, courage, humility, and many more. Character is not based upon, or determined by, your education, background, race, ancestors, or experiences in life. Each and every day, you are writing your internal script by choosing your values. Then, your script (resulting character based upon the values you have internalized) will dictate your decisions and responses in any given situation.

True character is revealed in times of adversity, pressure, and stress. When you squeeze a lemon what do you get? Lemon juice. The true nature of a lemon cannot be hidden, and the same is true for you.

In this book, you will discover 30 characteristics of very successful leaders and learn how to develop them. Are there more than 30? Yes, of course, but very few people are willing to read an encyclopedia of leadership, so I had to choose those I felt would be most relevant.

Developing these *"Leadership Gems"* will certainly help you develop your character, and thus increase your ability to influence (lead) others in every given situation.

Isn't that a bold claim? Absolutely. However, I make this statement with complete confidence. I know it's true because I have learned to apply them and achieved amazing results.

Some of these characteristics will come easier to you than others. You may be tempted to downplay the significance of those that don't come easy, but in truth, those are the ones you should focus on most. In terms of character, we should focus on developing weak areas. In terms of abilities, or competencies, we should focus on developing areas of strength. Character always compounds competency.

Leaders are like diamonds. They are unique and individual. No two are just alike. They are rare, very valuable, formed under pressure, and are very strong.

The word diamond comes from the Greek word *"adamas"* meaning tough, unbreakable, or indestructible. As my husband Mack says, *"Shiny objects get noticed. So do shiny people."*

Don't be afraid to shine bright in your areas of strength, but relative to your character, don't neglect to develop your areas of weakness. Brad Milford said, *"Gems are mined and discovered. They definitely can't shine without light. There is power in the light you draw in as well as what you radiate. The desire is for you to be brilliant."*

Now, let's start mining leadership gems.

CHAPTER ONE
BE AUTHENTIC

"The authentic self is the soul made visible."

~ Sarah Ban Breathnach

Authenticity is a paradox.

Merriam-Webster defines paradox as, *"…a person, situation, or action having seemingly contradictory qualities or phases."*

There is a paradox in authenticity because we all want authenticity in everything and everyone else, but we struggle to be authentic ourselves.

Authenticity requires us to be vulnerable. And, vulnerability is commonly, and incorrectly, perceived as a "weakness."

It's not a weakness. It's a great strength. Only a strong person can make visible his soul and be confidently unashamed of what is found there. Not because he is perfect, but because he acknowledges he is not, although he is striving to be better.

Because authenticity builds trust, it is priceless when it comes to relationships and leadership.

When it comes to influence, those who are genuine, real, honest, and upfront with us have a lot of influence with us because we know we can trust them. Their word is worth something because we know they are always honest. We may not always like what they have to say because sometimes the truth isn't easy to hear. But, we always value that we can count on it being truthful.

Authenticity requires a fine balance between tact and truth, but both should be respected equally. Being authentic is a choice to be true to your core values, your self, and to honor that in your relationships with other people.

Brené Brown said, *"Authenticity is a collection of choices that we have to make every day. It's about the choice to show up and be real. The choice to be honest. The choice to let our true selves be seen."*

There is an incredible amount of pressure on those who are in a formal leadership position to conform to society's standard of what an "ideal" leader looks and acts like. The "ideal" leader doesn't admit mistakes, doesn't get emotional, doesn't build relationships, isn't afraid of conflict, and doesn't have any problem balancing his or her role as parent, spouse, and person, with his or her role as manager, CEO, or business owner. The worst of it is the misconception that your role as a leader takes priority over your role as person.

To be blunt, that's B.S.

No, not that "B.S.," I mean it's a Belief System. And, it doesn't serve anyone. Who you are as a person defines who you are as a leader. Your greatest strength as a leader is to be true to yourself and let your own natural leadership style shine.

The most effective leaders have a greater natural inclination toward building a relationship with those they want to influence. That is an incredible strength. Regardless of who you are trying to lead, you will have more influence if they feel like you value them as a person. Remember, authenticity is a strength because it builds trust. Trust will always increase influence.

Dale Carnegie said, *"Influence is ultimately an outcropping of trust - the higher the trust, the greater the influence."*

My husband Mack always says, *"When you increase your influence, you increase your options."* So, increasing trust increases our leadership ability, which in turn increases the options we have available to us. We simply have to be intentional about being authentic in order to build trust.

LIVE AUTHENTICALLY

Look for ways to be more authentic in your daily life. If you aren't fine, don't tell others you are. Admit things aren't fantastic and ask for help, support, or even prayer. If you don't know the answer to a question, don't make it up or guess. Admit you don't know, ask for time to find the answer, and then ensure you follow up. If you don't agree with something, don't go along with it just to keep the peace. Work to intentionally resolve the issue through constructive dialogue.

True influence and leadership aren't based on appearing to be different than you are. It's based on your authenticity and your willingness to develop your character. That's what turns authenticity into a strength instead of a weakness.

Success isn't based on your ability to cover up your flaws. Success is based on your ability to overcome them.

We often are afraid to be authentic because we are afraid of being vulnerable. What if someone finds out we aren't perfect? What if someone realizes we make mistakes? What if someone realizes we are flawed, human, and don't have a Facebook perfect life? In truth, they already know it. None of us are perfect.

We all make mistakes and have weaknesses. We don't need anyone to tell us – we already know it. We know it about everyone else, and as much as we are afraid of them finding out, everyone already knows it about us. The question they have is, do we know it? We understand people aren't perfect. We don't expect them to be. We respect those who don't pretend to be.

CHAPTER TWO
BE PROACTIVE

"I am not a product of my circumstances. I am a product of my decisions."

~ Stephen R. Covey

If I asked a group of people to define "proactive," I would probably get a wide variety of responses such as: taking initiative, anticipating, preparing for, or taking control of. But, to be proactive, as Dr. Stephen R. Covey defines it, is to respond to any given situation based on values, instead of emotions.[1]

Being proactive is more than just taking action or initiative. It's recognizing, as humans, we have the unique capability to choose our response in any given situation. As Dr. Covey states, *"Our behavior is a function of our decisions, not our conditions. We can subordinate feelings to values. We have the initiative and the responsibility to make things happen."*

That's powerful – because it means regardless of what happens to you in life, you have the ability, and responsibility, to decide what you will think. How you think determines what you feel. How you feel determines what you do. What you do determines the results you get in life. The opposite of proactive is reactive, which means empowering something else to control you. Reactive people allow their physical environment, or external conditions, to control how they feel. They allow what happens on the outside to dictate how they feel on the inside.

External conditions can influence you, but they don't determine you. Life will happen. It won't always be easy, good, or fun. You might get sick. You may lose your job, get divorced, or lose a loved one. I hope your story isn't like mine, one of years of sexual abuse as a teenager. But, I'm certain you have or will experience adversity in life.

We all do.

Being proactive means choosing your response to what happens based on your values, instead of reacting based on your emotions. We've probably all made the mistake of blowing up in a situation, getting mad, and saying or doing something we later regret. We've probably all experienced a time when we empowered ourselves, rather than allowing something or someone else, to dictate our response. Maybe you've seen a friend or loved one who is terminally ill, suffering greatly, or handicapped, and yet rises above their circumstances with a positive spirit and incredible strength. It's not easy to do, but it does get easier the more you do it.

When we are proactive, we greatly increase the amount of influence we have with other people. Our ability to lead at a high level increases exponentially when we can first lead and influence ourselves well.

Years ago, I was searching for a candidate to fill an open position in my department at work. After many resumes, several interviews, and several months of searching, I found an extremely qualified person with relevant experience. She was a perfect fit for the position, was from out of town, and was relocating to be close to her future husband. We hired her.

A few weeks after she started work, she and I sat down together for a one-on-one training session. Uncharacteristically, she was disengaged during the session. Finally, realizing we weren't accomplishing anything, I pushed the computer screen away and I asked her what was on her mind.

"I'm not sure I can keep working here," she replied, breaking down into tears. *"My fiancé broke up with me because he was seeing someone else. I am thinking about moving back home since we aren't getting married."*

7

I was floored. After months of searching, rounds of interviews, and no small expense, I had gone to great lengths to hire her, train her, and now I was probably going to lose her. It would take several more months to replace her. I had about half a second to choose my response. I could be reactive based on my feelings of frustration and disappointment, or I could be proactive based on my values of helping her make the right decision for herself and respecting her trust and confidence in me. I replied, *"Whatever decision you need to make regarding moving back home or staying here, I will support you. If you decide to leave, I will give you a good reference based on your time here. If you decide to stay, I'll be happy to have you. You need to think about what is best for you right now. If this job isn't the answer, I'll help you find another one back home."*

That wasn't easy to say. I really wanted her to stay. But, I was able to be proactive. I realized, if she knew I supported her and cared about her either way, she would make the best decision for herself. If she made the best decision for herself, it would be the best decision, in the long run, for me and the organization. She chose to stay.

If being proactive is a challenge for you, look for ways to start being proactive in small ways. If your order gets messed up at the restaurant, remember everyone makes mistakes. You aren't perfect either. If you make a mistake at work, don't get angry. Search for the lesson in it. When it's raining, smile anyway. If your 16 year old daughter gets pregnant out of wedlock, choose to love her more.

Start by being proactive with small things, and the big things will become easier. Your influence with anyone and everyone will grow over time.

CHAPTER THREE
BE RESPONSIBLE

"The price of greatness is responsibility."

~ Winston Churchill

Being a leader, whether you are a formal leader, the boss, or a parent, comes with responsibilities. Most of us understand this on a broad level – to be a leader means to be a role model, set an example, etc. But, what does it really mean to be responsible or to take responsibility?

Jim Rohn said, *"Character isn't something you were born with and can't change, like your fingerprints. It's something you weren't born with and must take responsibility for forming."*

Taking responsibility as a leader means accepting responsibility for developing your own character and then helping someone else develop theirs. John C. Maxwell stated, *"Reaching your God-given potential requires taking responsibility for yourself and your life. It means taking an active leadership role with yourself."*

By reading this book, you have accepted that responsibility at one level. However, you must apply the principles and share them with others to increase your leadership to the next level.

If you don't accept that responsibility, you won't be able to become very successful as a leader or highly effective in any area of life for that matter. Let's look at two ways accepting responsibility improves leadership and increases influence:

RESPONSIBILITY TO OTHERS

As a leader and/or parent, spouse, co-worker, friend, etc., your first responsibility is *to* others. This is the foundation for influence. This means leadership of others starts with leadership of self. You can't lead anyone else at a high level if you aren't able to lead yourself well first because you can't give someone what you don't have.

Leadership isn't something you do. It's something you are. And, it starts inside you. We all have influence on some level, with some people. If we want to increase our influence to a higher level, impact more people, and create a greater legacy in the lives of others, we must start by accepting the responsibility for striving to be better ourselves. We must work to develop leadership qualities within ourselves first.

The responsibility *to* others comes when you are ready to say, *"I'll work on me first, so I can help you."* Until and unless you are ready to accept that responsibility, you won't be able to become a very successful leader.

Would you prefer to choose your vacation destination based on the advice of a tour guide or a travel agent? Advice from someone who has actually been there is much more valuable than advice from someone who has only seen the brochure. Being an effective leader of yourself before leading others is much the same.

RESPONSIBILITY FOR OTHERS

Although the first responsibility is foundational, and you can't influence many without it, the second responsibility is perhaps where you actually build more influence. Accepting responsibility is a give and take. First, you give: knowledge, credit when things go right, respect, love, help, coaching, opportunities and experiences, freedom, and through delegation, even responsibilities.

In other words, you nurture others and help them grow.

And, then you take: the blame, the responsibility when things don't go well, the burdens, the responsibility for removing roadblocks, their input, their feedback, and the time to listen. In other words, you become accountable. Rudy Giuliani wrote about this in his book, *Leadership,* and said, *"More than anyone, leaders should welcome being held accountable. Nothing builds confidence in a leader more than their willingness to take responsibility for what happens during their watch."* [1] In fact, he summarizes his entire leadership philosophy with a two-word sign that sits on his desk. It says, *"I'M RESPONSIBLE."*

The leader who will accept responsibility *to* and *for* others on the team, in the organization, or even in the family will very quickly increase his or her influence.

Ask yourself how you can accept or ask for additional responsibility in either your professional life or your personal life. At work, it could mean asking to take the lead on a new project or volunteering to lead a focus group. At church, it could mean starting a study group, so you can bring together a group of couples who want to increase their influence with their families. At home, it could mean becoming the leader by setting a good example with your food choices and helping your children or spouse do the same.

Accepting responsibility for everything in your life is the key to being able to change anything in your life. Accepting more responsibility in any area of your life will allow you to develop greater influence in that area of your life. More responsibility equals greater influence and control.

CHAPTER FOUR
BE POSITIVE

"Positive thinking will let you do everything better than negative thinking will."

~ Zig Ziglar

Now that you know you can choose your response, what response should you choose?

The first, and perhaps most important, is to choose to be positive. The choice to be positive isn't just important for you as a leader. It's important for you as a person. The value of positive thinking and the affect it will have on your leadership ability and your personal life cannot be overstated.

Choosing to be positive in some things is easy. It's easy to be positive and have a good attitude when everything is going your way.

However, to remain positive in *everything*, little things, big things, upsetting things, frustrating things, sad things, hurtful things, can be a challenge to even the most proactive person.

It's important to realize being positive when things are good doesn't really help you increase your influence and leadership with other people. Everyone expects you to be positive when things are going well. It's when things aren't going well that you have the greatest opportunity to demonstrate your leadership ability and increase your influence.

Obstacles and problems are real. There have been and always will be situations you cannot control. What you can control is your mental stance, or your decision to see the situation positively or negatively. A negative mental stance creates negative results and will decrease your influence with everyone around you. A positive mental stance creates positive results and increases your influence with everyone around you. How you think about your problems and obstacles determines what you do about them.

Staying positive doesn't mean you are unrealistic. Having a positive attitude is a character trait, something you must cultivate in yourself even when things aren't going well. It doesn't mean avoiding the facts or pretending they aren't there. It does mean choosing to be positive in spite of the facts.

You can intentionally create more positivity in your relationships, at work, at home, with family, and in your life. Creating more positivity will leverage your leadership.

When you are positive, you inspire hope in others. You remind them to look for the good and find the bright side. Those who are positive inspire us. Those who inspire us have more influence with us.

Creating more positivity is as limitless as your imagination. But, it won't happen by accident, especially if you are going through a difficult time.

Several years ago, there was a popular slogan among many churches. It was called *"WWJD"* and encouraged people, especially youth, to ask themselves, *"What Would Jesus Do?"* There was a movement to wear bracelets with "WWJD" stamped on them, so the wearer would always be reminded to respond how they thought Jesus might respond. Being positive is very similar because you can ask yourself *"What would a positive person do?"* And, if you want to be proactive, you can choose the positive response.

Even if you feel like you are a positive person already, there is always an opportunity to be more positive. Consider what you say, how you think, what you worry about, and what you decide not to worry about. Most of our worry is unfounded anyway. Start by intentionally choosing to be more positive in these three areas:

THOUGHTS

Every morning when I wake up, one of my first thoughts is to consider what's on my agenda for the day. Then, I ask myself, *"What opportunities will come my way today?"* Regardless of what's on your agenda for the day, you can think about it positively or negatively. *"I have to go to work today"* is negative. *"I get to go to work today"* is positive. It's the same job. What's different is your attitude toward the job.

WORDS

Get rid of any negative phrases from your vocabulary. I mean it. All of them. Eliminate all words that are negative. Remove any phrases like *"I'm afraid…"* or *"I can't…"* or *"I have to…"* It may seem small, but as Norman Vincent Peale said, *"Mighty oaks grow from little acorns."*

ACTIONS

If you want positivity in your life, read positive books. Watch inspirational movies. Talk to positive people. Volunteer to help someone. If something is a negative influence in your life, get rid of it. It's not serving you. You may need to change your situation, your job, or even your friends. That doesn't mean you don't love them, but it does mean you don't accept their influence.

CHAPTER FIVE
BE RESILIENT

"The greatest glory in living lies not in never falling, but in rising every time we fall."

~ Nelson Mandela

Resilience. Just the word makes you want to sit up a little taller or lift your head a little higher. Resilience is the ability to recover, to spring back, to thrive, and to become strong after, or in spite of, tough times. Resilience is one of the qualities we admire most in other people and expect most in our leaders.

I learned far too young that life isn't fair. Raised on an isolated farm in Alabama, I was sexually abused by my father from age 12 – 19. I was dressed up, photographed nude, beaten, tied up, raped, emotionally blackmailed, and psychologically abused. I was forced to play the role of a wife and even shared with other men due to my father's perversions.

Desperate to escape, I left home at 19 without a job, a car, or even a high school diploma.

I have never looked back. When I left, I realized I had a choice. I could choose to be resilient and overcome what happened to me. Or, I could let it drag me down for the rest of my life.

Some people master resiliency at an early age, while others may not find it until old age. Some never find it. Some people learn to be resilient to some circumstances, but not others. As the leader, it's your job to be resilient. That's why you were chosen to lead.

Followers look to leaders to be strong, bounce back from adversity, and help them overcome challenges as well. The question isn't whether we will experience adversity in life, but rather when? You have already overcome some challenges to get to where you are today. That may be the reason you're reading this book and striving to improve yourself.

In life, there are two choices: move forward or move backward. To remain still is not a choice. You are either choosing to intentionally move forward or automatically moving backward.

Refusing to choose is a choice. We choose to be resilient because to choose otherwise is to choose to move backward. Regardless of what happens, we make a decision to get up, dust ourselves off, and try again.

When you choose to be resilient, you increase your influence with those who are following you. You also may increase your influence and leadership with someone who isn't (yet) following but *is watching* to see what kind of leader you are based on the choices you make.

I talk to many people who have been through adversity of all kinds. Illness, death of a loved one, abuse, domestic violence, loss of a job, loss of security, loss of faith, and more. I'm no longer surprised by the depth of pain we suffer. What I find impressive is how resilient some of us are.

Rick Warren, author of the very popular book, *The Purpose Driven Life,* wrote this about resilience, *"We are products of our past, but we don't have to be prisoners of it."* [1]

How fast and how quickly we rise to resilience is determined by our Resilience Factor, which is our ability to move beyond surviving to thriving. The higher our Resilience Factor, the greater our ability to overcome whatever happens to us in life.

What I've discovered is there is one fundamental difference between the people who are able to overcome adversity of any type and those who are not: Attitude. Yes, life is tough. There is no doubt you either have in the past, currently face, or will at some point experience trials in life. Each trial we face is a mountain when we're climbing it. Only when we get to the top are we able to see what's on the other side and the possibilities that lie ahead.

Attitude is the key difference between those who find the strength to keep going and those who decide to turn back. I've already mentioned being positive relative to *how* we think about a situation. But to truly be resilient, we also must choose *what* we are thinking about.

After I left home at 19, I had to become resilient to thrive and bounce back. I had to learn to change my thoughts. To change my thoughts, I had to change the *way* I was thinking and *what* I was thinking. In all transparency, it took me many years to truly be able to thrive, and it's something I still work hard at every day. I couldn't thrive by dwelling on all the pain from my past. I had to focus my thoughts forward on the future.

Change what you are thinking about. Rather than focus on the problem, seek the solution. Ask yourself three empowering questions: *What can I do? How can I do it? Who can help me?*

Mary Holloway said, *"Resilience is knowing that you are the only one that has the power and responsibility to pick yourself up."*

Resilient leaders realize they can't control everything. But, they also realize they can control some things, and they realize they should only focus on what they can control. You will never be able to fix everything. But, you can change some things. And, you can always change yourself.

CHAPTER SIX
BE COURAGEOUS

"Courage always comes with the sun. You can conquer almost any fear if you will only make up your mind to do so. For remember, fear doesn't exist anywhere except in your mind."

~ Dale Carnegie

Often, we think of courage as being brave in the face of adversity, fear, or danger. Our heroes are brave: the firefighter who rushes into a burning building to rescue a child or the medical flight team that flies bravely into a storm to transport an accident victim. But, courage is more than that. Courage is the will to stand up and do the right thing, even when it's not the easy thing.

Life (and leadership) is full of challenges. It takes courage to meet them head on and come out victorious on the other side. We are called to be brave, even when we are just as fearful as those who are following us.

It's not that leaders don't feel fear. They feel it too but have learned to overcome it with courage. When we overcome fear with courage, we inspire everyone else to do the same. As Billy Graham once stated, *"Courage is contagious. When a brave man takes a stand, the spines of others are often stiffened."*

It takes courage to resign from a good paying job when you realize the company isn't ethical. It takes courage to learn something new and get outside of your comfort zone. It takes courage to admit your character flaws and intentionally work to improve them.

Fear is something we create with our thoughts. In the words of Dale Carnegie, *"...Fear doesn't exist anywhere except in your mind."* That's why different people have different fears – because they think differently.

I am often asked if I'm ever afraid before I speak to a large group. Most people have a fear of speaking in public, so they assume everyone else has the same fear.

That's not true however. I'm not afraid of speaking in public because I'm not afraid of making a mistake. I already know I'm not perfect, and I don't pretend to be. So, there is no reason for me to be afraid of speaking in public. The worst that can happen is that I make a mistake, and I'm prepared for that.

Everyone faces fear. The question is, what will we do about it? Nelson Mandela said *"I learned that courage was not the absence of fear, but the triumph over it. The brave man is not he who does not feel afraid, but he who conquers that fear."*

Fear is the emotion we create when we think worried thoughts. We create fear by telling ourselves all the bad things that can happen. And, what we focus on expands. To be courageous and overcome fear, we must identify a reason to move forward that is stronger than our fear. This comes down to our core values and allowing them to guide us, rather than emotions of worry, concern, or fear.

The vast majority of our fears are completely unfounded anyway. Robert Leahy, in his book *The Worry Cure,* [1] cites a statistic that 85% of what we are afraid of never happens.

Disclaimer – this does not include appropriate fears which drive sensible behavior. If you see a large, poisonous snake on the path while you are out hiking, it's perfectly appropriate to be afraid of getting bit. That is a valid concern. Act accordingly. Refusing to take appropriate action when there is truly a dangerous situation isn't bravery – it's stupidity. Let's look at how very successful leaders overcome fear to be courageous.

IDENTIFY YOUR FEAR

When you find yourself not taking action or not

moving forward, take the time to really think about why. There may be many things you're afraid of. Fear of failure. Fear of making a mistake. Fear of not being popular. Fear that others may not agree with your decision. Dr. Stephen Covey referred to the *"Circle of Concern,"* where everything you can't control or influence is placed. If you venture into the *"Circle of Concern,"* you are simply wasting valuable time and energy.

IDENTIFY WHAT YOU CAN CONTROL

Once you have identified your fear, quit thinking about it. Instead, make a list of everything you can control, influence, or cause to happen instead. This is where truly successful leaders spend their time and energy – on the things they *can* do. If you focus your time, energy, and effort on the things you can control, you will find over time there will be less things in your *"Circle of Concern."*

TAKE ACTION

If the situation is out of your control, there isn't any reason to worry about it. Not moving forward at all or never taking a risk isn't an option for very successful leaders. They see mistakes as learning opportunities, failures as strength builders, and the unknown as potential for positive things. As Muhammad Ali said, *"He who is not courageous enough to take risks will accomplish nothing in life."*

CHAPTER SEVEN
BE PURPOSE DRIVEN

"The purpose of life is a life of purpose."

~ Robert Byrne

Purpose in life gives us meaning. Purpose provides us direction and a true north for aligning our time, energy, and efforts. In the words of Helen Keller, *"Many persons have a wrong idea of what constitutes true happiness. It is not attained through self-gratification but through fidelity to a worthy purpose."*

When we are living in alignment with our purpose, life has significance, great joy, and meaning. Each day is exciting and filled with beautiful opportunity, even if your circumstances aren't good or what you want them to be. Purpose unleashes potential, possibility, and passion.

We are all familiar with the term "mid-life crisis." Odds are good, you know someone who has been through a mid-life crisis. One day they woke up, evaluated their life up to that point and realized it was lacking in one dimension or another. Maybe, they realized their career goals hadn't been achieved. Maybe, they realized they weren't happy in their marriage. Or maybe, it was an identity crisis where they felt like life had no purpose, meaning, or value.

Not everyone goes through a "mid-life crisis" and gets a divorce, buys a red sports car, or walks out on a successful career to find themselves by hitchhiking across America. But, many people do experience a paradigm shift where they wake up one day and realize they are just "going through the motions." Activities are no longer fun. Work has become dull. Relationships have lost their flavor. The zest of life is gone.

It might be gradual or sudden, but it's a realization that life lacks joy, purpose, meaning, and direction.

If you have never experienced a "mid-life crisis"

yourself, you can avoid it by identifying your purpose and aligning your life with it.

If you have experienced a "mid-life crisis" or are experiencing it now, you can begin to focus your life by identifying your purpose and aligning your life with it.

Living your life "purpose driven" creates meaning. You don't have to wonder *"Why am I here?"* because you already know your purpose. Being purpose driven simplifies your life. If you know what your purpose is, you can say *"yes"* to the opportunities that are in alignment and say *"no"* to the opportunities that aren't. You can simply ask yourself, *"Is this the best use of my time?"* when you know what *your* standard is. Of course, we all have a different purpose and different gifts that serve our purpose. What's in alignment for you will not necessarily be what's in alignment for others.

It takes discipline to be purpose driven, but your leadership ability is multiplied when you are leading others from a strong foundation centered on your purpose. People follow those who know where they are going and why they are going there. No one wants to follow a lost leader. Until you know where you are going and why you are going there, it will be difficult to influence anyone else to come with you.

Rick Warren said, *"My ultimate goal…is for you to live the life you're intended to live."*

Your personal definition of success is based on your core values, which are derived from your purpose. When you know your purpose, and let that be *the* driving force in your life, you will achieve success because you know where you are, where you're going, and how you're going to get there.

There was a famous scene in Lewis Carroll's *Alice in Wonderland* where Alice asked the Cheshire cat which road to take. *"Where do you want to go?"* the cat asked. *"I don't know."* Alice replied. *"Then it doesn't matter which road you take."* the cat said as it grinned and faded away.

If you don't know where you're going, you will never get there.

John F. Kennedy said, *"Efforts and courage are not enough without purpose and direction."* No one has ever become very successful without knowing and living his purpose.

To get started, spend some quiet time thinking about your values. It will require some soul searching relative to what's most important to you and why. It takes time. Journal and reflect on what your strengths are, what you are good at, or times when you shined. What makes you come alive? What do you dream about? What do you cry about?

I have several exercises that can help you identify your purpose, personal mission, and vision for your life in my book, *PRIME Time: The Power of Effective Planning* if you want to go deeper, but journaling is the best place to start.

You can also ask someone close to you or a trusted mentor to help you. Either way, don't take it lightly. Your life is a stewardship of your talents, abilities, and gifts. Use them wisely. Rick Warren, in his book *The Purpose Driven Life,* suggests it's a spiritual journey.

Like any journey, it will take time. Once you have identified your purpose, you will continue to refine it if you continue to intentionally grow, personally and professionally.

CHAPTER EIGHT
BE PASSIONATE

"There are many things that will catch my eye, but there are only a few that catch my heart…It is those I consider to pursue."
~ Tim Redmond

Leaders who achieve great things have passion. They make things happen. You cannot achieve something extraordinary without passion. Passion is the spark that will ignite your soul and fuel your energy long beyond the point where you would have otherwise quit.

Passion is what separates someone who is achieving greatness and excellence from someone who is just doing a good job. When you are passionate about something, you will not hesitate to sacrifice things of lesser value in order to achieve it. Those who are truly passionate and living their purpose know nearly everything is of lesser value when compared to what they are passionate about.

You can't buy passion. It's priceless.

Leaders who are passionate inspire others to work harder, dream bigger, and reach their own potential. People want to follow a passionate leader who cares about what they are doing and why they are doing it.

Once you identify your cause and your passion and align that with your calling and purpose everything else will fall into place. You won't have to worry about finding a "job" because you will be living your dream.

If your passion is to be a stay at home parent and your spouse supports that passion, it will be easy to be the best parent in the world for your children. You won't mind sacrificing sleep to stay up with a sick little one. You won't mind baking cookies for the cheer squad or making endless trips to little league. You will love it!

If your passion is to build your own company, it will be easy to put your life savings into starting the business. You won't mind staying up until midnight to work on the business plan or learning to design your own website. You won't care that you spend your "spare" time networking and building your business instead of hanging out with friends. You will love making it happen!

You probably won't have trouble identifying what you are passionate about. Whatever excites you, makes you happy, makes you smile, gives you energy, and whatever you enjoy doing so much you would pay to do it is what you are passionate about.

Some people know what they are passionate about from a very young age; others may take years to discover their passion.

Your passion and life's work should be in alignment with your purpose. Sure, you can be passionate about something that isn't in alignment with your purpose, but that's called a hobby, not a calling. Teaching group fitness is a hobby for me, not a calling. I am passionate about it, but it's not my life's work and calling. Therefore, I dedicate only a proportionate amount of my time and energy doing it. Make sure you clearly differentiate your hobbies from your purpose.

PASSION PRODUCES ENERGY

When you are passionate, you will work much longer and harder than if you aren't excited about what you are doing. That's why entrepreneurs often don't mind working seven days a week. They enjoy what he is doing, and doesn't consider it "work." Confucius said, *"If you love what you do, you will never work another day in your life."*

PASSION INSPIRES OTHERS

Ken Hemphill said, *"Vision does not ignite growth, passion does. Passion fuels vision, and vision is the focus of the power of passion. Leaders who are passionate about their call create vision."* Passion is contagious. It's exciting. It attracts others to you. When other people feel your passion for your vision, they will get behind you and help you turn it into reality. Far too many people settle in life. Those who don't settle for average, routine, or comfortable have fire, enthusiasm, and joy in their daily lives. They inspire many others to follow. They give us hope that life doesn't have to be dull or boring. As Nelson Mandela said, *"There is no passion to be found in playing small - in settling for a life that is less than the one you are capable of living."*

PASSION UNLEASHES POTENTIAL

According to Jean De La Fontaine, *"Man is so made that whenever anything fires his soul, impossibilities vanish."* When you are passionate about what you are doing, you are far more likely to be successful because you will be more determined. There are many roadblocks on the road to success. You must be determined in order to navigate them and reach your potential.

Passion enables you to say *"no"* to the good, so you can say *"yes"* to the great. Passionate leaders don't settle for average, easy, routine, or comfortable. As Norman Vincent Peale said, (they) *"shoot for the moon and, even if they miss, land among the stars."*

CHAPTER NINE
BE CONFIDENT

"Believe in yourself! Have faith in your abilities! Without a humble but reasonable confidence in your own powers you cannot be successful or happy."

~ Norman Vincent Peale

Confidence is the foundation on which very successful leaders build their influence. If the foundation is weak, the structure will collapse under stress. Confidence is crucial to success in life and leadership because confidence builds trust.

Confidence sends an unspoken message of experience, strength, certainty, and success. We want to follow leaders who demonstrate confidence. Oscar de la Renta stated, *"The qualities I most admire…are confidence and kindness."*

Leaders without confidence have weak followers. After all, if you don't trust yourself, why would anyone else? As Vince Lombardi said, *"Confidence is contagious. So is lack of confidence."*

There are two basic kinds of confidence: self-confidence and situational-confidence.

Self-confidence is conviction of your values and core beliefs enhanced by experience and lessons learned from both successes and failures. In other words, self-confidence is static. The factors that make you uniquely you create your self-confidence. Self-confidence is developed over time. While other people can support you, self-confidence will only be realized by growing and developing your own character.

Situational-confidence is certainty in the outcome of a situation which is enhanced by your knowledge, skills, and abilities. In other words, situational-confidence is dynamic and is affected by factors outside of your control. Situational-confidence can be increased by developing your competency.

You won't always have situational-confidence. There will be times when you try something new, take on a new job, or first become a manager and lack experience or technical knowledge. There will be times when you have a new relationship with a team member and lack confidence in their ability to get the job done.

You may have self-confidence because it's based on your character which remains the same in every situation but lack situational-confidence. For example, you may lack situational-confidence, perhaps in a new job, and still have plenty of self-confidence in your ability to learn.

That shows strength of character because it takes self-confidence to develop situational-confidence. The more self-confidence you have (without arrogance), the greater success and influence you will have as a leader.

It's important to note confidence must be balanced with humility to avoid arrogance. Confident leaders inspire trust. Arrogant leaders destroy it.

To develop more situational-confidence, focus on developing your knowledge, skills, talents, and abilities. Situational-confidence may also increase with time and experience.

To develop more self-confidence, work on identifying and improving your character weaknesses. As Nicole Scherzinger noted, *"Confidence comes with maturity, being more accepting of yourself."* Find a mentor to hold you accountable. Ask a trusted friend to help you identify character issues: lack of integrity, not making or keeping commitments, lack of humility, not taking ownership of mistakes, making too much of your mistakes, etc. Develop a personal growth plan to keep you on track.

Confident people become confident leaders. Make it

a point to identify areas where you lack self-confidence. Then, determine what you need to work on internally. Who you are on the inside is what determines your results on the outside.

CHARACTERISTICS OF CONFIDENCE

Confident Leaders:	**Unconfident Leaders:**
Aren't afraid to take risks	Are afraid to take action
Aren't afraid of making mistakes	Are afraid of failure
Aren't afraid of leading others	Are looking for someone to lead them
Aren't afraid of trusting instincts	Are unable to make a decision until they have "all the facts"
Aren't afraid of being persistent	Are prone to giving up too easily
Aren't afraid of being passionate	Are easily distracted from their mission
Aren't afraid of learning something new	Are worried about not always having the answer
Aren't afraid of empowering others	Are afraid of giving away authority
Aren't afraid of taking a stand	Are willing to sacrifice values
Aren't afraid of following someone else	Are afraid of not having control

CHAPTER TEN
BE REALISTIC

"You have to pay a price. You will find that everything in life exacts a price, and you will have to decide whether the price is worth the prize."

~ Sam Nunn

Merriam-Webster defines realistic as: *"Concern for fact or reality."*

You must see a situation clearly to act appropriately.

Achievable goals, outcomes, and results are always based on reality. We have a responsibility to others to make our decisions based on facts, not fantasies.

Rudy Ruettiger said, *"Reality...is the enemy of fantasies but not of dreams."*

Whether it's setting a realistic strategic goal for your company or creating a realistic budget for your family, you must first honestly evaluate the situation, circumstances, and people involved, and then decide to be positive about it. Being "optimistically realistic" requires a fine balance.

Yes, you can do just about anything you decide to do, if it's physically possible. Gabby Douglas overcame the fact that she didn't start formal gymnastics training until she was six years old. Most successful gymnasts start between two and three years old. However, Gabby went on to win multiple gold medals in the Olympics. It was possible, and she made it happen.

You can accomplish incredible things when you are determined enough to do so. But, the price may be more than you are willing to pay.

You must be realistic about where you are starting and where you want to go before you can decide if the price you must pay is worth it.

As James Russell Lowell said, *"No one can produce great things who is not thoroughly sincere in dealing with himself."*

You must consider where you have been, where you are now, and where you want to go in order to be very successful and effective. As John C. Maxwell said, *"Every time you want to learn something, you must be able to take the new thing you've learned today and build upon what you learned yesterday to keep growing. That's the only way to gain traction and keep improving yourself."*

Take time and reflect on a regular basis to raise your self-awareness. Consider your strengths, weaknesses, goals, direction, and dreams. Be realistic about the path you must take to reach the latter and what will be required.

Sharpen your strengths and improve your weaknesses. Remember, work *in* your strength zone when it comes to your talents and abilities, and work *on* your weaknesses when it comes to your character.

Strengths related to talents and abilities will allow you to accomplish great things because you are gifted in those areas. But, weaknesses of character will prevent you from accomplishing great things because character weakness is a stumbling block. Gabby Douglas is naturally very talented as an athlete, but she had to have great discipline (strength of character) in order to maximize her potential as an athlete. If she had lacked discipline, regardless of her natural talents and abilities, she would have never achieved the same results.

Being realistic will help you maintain an important perspective when you make a mistake. It will keep you from over-exaggerating the impact of your mistake and help you learn a lesson from the mistake. A good way to maximize the benefit of the potential lesson is to constructively consider what you should have done different or what you will do different in the future rather than criticizing yourself for making the mistake.

Being realistic about yourself, goals, strengths, and weaknesses will allow you to become more successful as a person.

Being realistic about other people and their strengths and weaknesses will allow you to become very effective as a leader.

Peter Marshall said, *"Give to us clear vision that we may know where to stand and what to stand for."*

As a leader, it's important to clearly and realistically cast the vision – and then help your team see it, believe it, and achieve it.

Be aware of the strengths of your team members in order to allow them opportunities to shine where they are gifted. It's also important to be aware of the weaknesses of your team members, so you can support them, help them grow, and also balance their weakness with someone who is strong in that area.

Be realistic about the situations you experience day to day, and be realistic about the progress you can make relative to your goals, big and small. With some people and some projects, progress will be slow. Be realistic.

Realistically, small steps can lead to big results over time. Being realistic about small gains will help you keep a long-term mindset and allow you to have patience. Dr. Henry Cloud said, *"The biggest enemy of the small-steps-big-results principle is our craving for having it all...All or nothing thinking keeps people stuck in destructive ruts. All success is built and sustained just like a building is built, one brick at a time."*

CHAPTER ELEVEN
BE INTENTIONAL

"Intentional living is the art of making our own choices before others' choices make us."

~ Richie Norton

No great achievement ever happened by accident. Great cathedrals weren't built in one day, great companies didn't just happen, and no one became very successful by mistake. Major accomplishments, and even most minor ones, only came about through dedicated, focused, *intentional* effort toward a goal. Hard work. And, lots of it.

Whatever it is you must do to move forward, at work, at home, and in life, you must be intentional about doing it consistently. You don't have to do it all in one day, (in fact, you can't) but you must do it every day.

If you aren't intentional you will find, if you haven't already, that you never seem to quite accomplish any of your goals. Life just gets in the way. At some point, you simply settle for not reaching your goal, dream, or destination.

Some people are simply content to drift through life, settling on a career that doesn't inspire them, settling on a spouse they are not happy with, or living an "average" life. We all have an opportunity to live a life of significance right where we are *if* we live life on purpose.

When it comes to stewardships, being intentional with your time, energy, talent, and your life is perhaps the greatest stewardship of all. It's also key to becoming very successful and highly effective as a leader. You don't have to be in a formal leadership position. In fact, most of the people who have made a huge impact on the world weren't in a formal leadership position. Mother Teresa wasn't. Yet even today, her legacy lives on. If you live with intention, you make a difference right where you are, and you will greatly increase your influence and leadership with others as you do so. To live a life that isn't intentional is to throw away your God-given potential.

There are four key areas in which you must be intentional if you want to increase your influence as a leader and become very successful:

ADD VALUE TO YOURSELF

You must be intentional about developing yourself in order to continue to grow. Carefully consider the books you read, the mentors you allow to give you advice, the influences you allow into your mind, and even the people you spend your free time with. Are those things helping you grow? Are they adding value to you as a person and as a leader? You cannot give someone what you don't have. Take every opportunity to add value to yourself, so you can add value to others. Part of my personal growth plan is reading 50 personal growth and leadership development books every year. As Benjamin Franklin said, *"Without continual growth and progress, such words as improvement, achievement, and success have no meaning."*

ADD VALUE TO OTHERS

Be intentional about adding value to someone else each and every day. Volunteer to help someone. People always remember the first person who offers to help. Every encounter you have is an opportunity to build your influence. If you are adding value to that person, you are building your influence with them and increasing your leadership skills. You are also contributing to their success which will help build your success. Zig Ziglar said, *"You can have everything in life you want, if you will just help other people get what they want."*

SAY YES

Be intentional about identifying what's truly important to you. Then, say *"yes"* only to the things aligned with your vision and mission. Fill your calendar, schedule, and your life based on *your* priorities. Ask yourself what you need to do in order to develop and enhance your leadership skills. Then, say *"yes"* to those things. If your priority is to be a better parent, say *"yes"* to things that allow you to become a better mom or dad. If your priority is to become a better team leader, say *"yes"* to growth and development opportunities in that area. What you say yes to defines your life.

SAY NO

If what you say yes to defines your life, what you say no to defines your legacy. You cannot do everything. Once you have determined what you will say yes to, learn to say *"no"* to everything else. Telling people *"no"* in a way that increases your leadership and influence with them isn't easy. According to Tony Blair, *"The art of leadership is saying no, not saying yes. It is very easy to say yes."* However, people will respect that you have priorities and aren't willing to compromise them. Saying *"yes"* to everything will derail your leadership – and your life. Saying *"no"* creates the space to say *"yes."*

CHAPTER TWELVE
BE DISCIPLINED

"In reading the lives of great men, I found that the first victory they won was over themselves. Self-discipline with all of them came first."
~ Harry Truman

You set your intentions for your life and leadership in chapter 11. Now, comes the more difficult part – living it. Setting a goal is always the easiest part of achieving it. Discipline is, quite frankly, a lot of work. It's not any fun. It's difficult and sometimes even painful. However, discipline shapes our character and makes us who we are. We are leaders because of who we are, not because of what we try to be.

Discipline means leading yourself well. As my favorite leadership author, Mack Story, said, *"If we can't lead ourselves well, we don't deserve to lead others at all."*

Discipline of self is the key to earning influence with others because our actions shout louder than words ever can. How we live is far more convincing than what we say. You must be intentional to identify your values. You must be disciplined to live them.

As any championship winning athlete will tell you, discipline often means doing the work when you don't feel like doing it. Sir Edmund Hillary said, *"It is not the mountains we conquer, but ourselves."*

START SMALL AND GROW FROM THERE

The best way to start becoming more disciplined is to start with a small task and accomplish it. When you set a goal or task for yourself and successfully reach it, you are building a successful track record which will help you create momentum for something bigger. When you set and keep commitments to yourself, you are also building your personal integrity account. Anytime you make a commitment to yourself and don't keep it, you are destroying your personal credibility with yourself and making it less likely that you will keep future commitments. You want to build credibility by setting small, easy to achieve goals to start with. Then, build up over time. You may not be able to commit with integrity to losing 10 pounds this month because you have tried before and failed. But maybe, you can commit with integrity to eating a salad today instead of a burger and fries.

JUST DO IT

Don't wait or put off doing something because the longer you wait, the more difficult it will become to actually do it. If you need to have a difficult conversation with an employee – do it now. If you've been putting off a chore around the house, take care of it, rather than waiting. Do it now.

Discipline is a "mind muscle." Just like your physical muscles, the more you exercise it, the stronger it becomes. Mark Twain suggested, *"Do something every day that you don't want to do. This is the golden rule for acquiring the habit of doing your duty without pain."*

CREATE A DEADLINE

We probably all have a little bit of a tendency to procrastinate on doing something we aren't excited about. It's easy to push it to the bottom of your to-do list when you don't want to do it, and there's no definite deadline for getting it done. If that's the case, give yourself a definite deadline and make it public. Make sure it's reasonable of course. Research has shown we are much more likely to accomplish goals when they are reasonable, measurable, and dated.

ELIMINATE DISTRACTIONS

One thing I have learned about discipline is if there is something I don't want to do, it's very easy to find excuses not to do it. So, I deliberately minimize or eliminate distractions to make it easier for myself. I turn off notifications on my phone at times because I need to focus on writing a chapter or a blog. It's all too easy to see an email pop up, and it leads to checking LinkedIn messages, Facebook notifications, Twitter hits, etc. Before I know it, 20 minutes have disappeared from my life, and all I've really done is avoided doing what needed to be done. Something I find helpful is to keep a notepad by my computer. If I get an idea or remember I need to do something, I write it down as a "do next," so I won't forget. Most importantly, I don't have to interrupt what I'm working on and avoid being distracted.

GAIN STRENGTH FROM ANOTHER AREA

If you want more discipline in one area of your life, it can help to create more discipline in other areas of your life. Much like starting small creates momentum, so does achieving other goals. This is why I set a physical goal each year, such as running a marathon. I'm intentionally creating more discipline in my physical life, and that will help me be more disciplined in other areas of life. Success in one area can create momentum in other areas.

CHAPTER THIRTEEN
BE INSPIRED

"You can't get much done in life if you only work on the days when you feel good."

~ Jerry West

Have you ever attended a conference or a seminar and felt really motivated to change something? Maybe, it was a conference on time management, and you decided from then on to live life by the perfect calendar. Maybe, it was a motivational speaker who inspired you and motivated you to "live your best life" or "accomplish any goal." Nearly all of us have had a similar experience where we attend an event, get fired up, but then come home to reality the next day.

The motivation slowly drains away in the whirlwind of life, and over time, your ability to see the goal fades away. Motivation is external – it comes from the outside. Inspiration comes from within. Because motivation is external, it can't and won't last. That's why you must be motivated regularly! In fact, Zig Ziglar said, *"People often say that motivation doesn't last. Well, neither does bathing – that's why we recommend it daily."*

We are focusing here on being inspired on the inside, so *you* can motivate others from the outside because you can't give someone what you don't have.

As Robin Sharma stated simply, *"Leadership is not about a title or a designation. It's about impact, influence, and inspiration."*

When you are committed to doing something, you must be able to clearly tap into *why* you are doing it. If you tap into *why* you are doing it, you will find the inspiration to keep doing it even when the new wears off, it's not exciting anymore, or it's not easy to do.

Simon Sinek, in his book *Start with Why,* wrote about how great leaders inspire others to take action when they

"Start with why." He states, *"People don't buy what you do, they buy why you do it."* [1]

The same concept applies for ourselves. If we focus on *why* we are doing something instead of *what* we are doing, we'll be inspired to continue doing it even when the going gets tough. And, the going will most likely get tough if it's something you are truly striving to achieve.

Everyone has days and decisions that aren't so easy. Your role as a leader comes with responsibility to and for others.

When you can keep the vision of what you are working for clearly in front of you, you will find the energy to do the tough things and make the tough decisions. That's why it's so important to be purpose driven.

Inspiration gives us hope. Hope gives us the vision of something better. The vision of something better gives us energy to keep going.

As a leader, you must be inspired because *you* are the example. Others are looking to *you* as their role model. Do you only work when you feel good? Remember, energy and attitude are contagious, and people follow leaders who are inspired, not expired.

Discover and tap into your "why" to stay inspired. Here are some other ways to help you stay inspired as a leader:

LEARN SOMETHING NEW

At the end of each day, I love to ask myself, *"What did I learn today?"* It seems like a very small thing, but learning something new each day will help you stay inspired.

VISIT INSPIRATIONAL PLACES

If you want to find inspiration through experiences, visit inspiring places. The Grand Canyon, Niagara Falls, and even your local park are all places to get outside and be inspired by nature. Visit historical sites or unique places in your home town to become inspired by them.

READ INSPIRATIONAL BOOKS

Read a great biography of someone interesting. Take advantage of your local bookstore or library and browse until you discover books you find inspirational. If you are filling your mind with inspirational wisdom from others, it will be very difficult to not become inspired.

WATCH INSPIRATIONAL MOVIES

Sure, some sappy love story may be fun to watch, but the truly inspirational movies are the ones that are based on true stories. You can't help but be inspired when you see someone else overcoming their obstacles. You will often find the strength to overcome your own.

DO SOMETHING

The famous boxer Muhammad Ali stated, *"I hated every minute of training, but I said, 'Don't quit. Suffer now and live the rest of your life as a champion.'"* In other words, he stayed inspired by remembering *why* he was working so hard. He took action even when he didn't feel like taking action.

CHAPTER FOURTEEN
BE MOTIVATIONAL

"Most of the things worth doing in the world had been declared impossible before they were done."

~ Louis Brandeis

Joshua Encarnacion was a young student athlete in college with an opportunity to play football. However, after his freshman year, he was diagnosed with atrial fibrillation. His dreams of playing football through college and beyond ended with that diagnosis. Struggling to find his identity and redefine himself, he was given an opportunity to be part of the student leadership body.

Unfortunately, this role ended abruptly too when the campus police showed up at a party he was hosting. He lost his student leadership role and was nearly expelled from college.

Joshua shared the struggles from that period of his life in a powerful TEDx talk in 2015. He shared what he learned from the experience – we have traditionally defined belief as something that is conditional and based upon someone meeting our expectations. That is, belief in someone has been defined as trust, faith, and confidence.

He proposes belief in someone should be redefined as encouragement, empowerment, and engagement because this definition doesn't involve judging anyone.

For high level leaders, this latter definition of belief comes much easier. When we are relationship oriented and naturally have more empathy, it's easier to believe in someone in a way that is unconditional and not judgmental. In Joshua's words, it's a "selfless" definition of belief. It's exactly how a parent believes, or should believe, in his or her children: unconditionally.

We should believe in our team members this way too. As the leader, it's our job to believe in others unconditionally. When we believe in someone unconditionally, we are able to encourage them, empower them, and engage them. In other words, we are able motivate them. And, as Norman Ralph Augustine said, *"Motivation will almost always beat mere talent."*

True motivation can only be accomplished when the other person knows and, most importantly, feels you have *their* best interest at heart. If they feel you are trying to motivate them for *your* benefit, they will feel manipulated instead of motivated.

We've all been in a situation where a salesperson is trying too hard to make the sale. We feel they are only interested in making a sale, so they can get the commission. Odds are, you ended up walking away without purchasing the product because you felt manipulated. Make sure whoever you are motivating understands why you want to motivate them and how they too will benefit.

None of us want to be manipulated. Manipulation destroys trust. You can't be effective as a leader if there is little or no trust in the relationship.

As the leader, to motivate others you should:

ENCOURAGE THEM

Encouraging someone is a selfless act. It means focusing on them, rather than yourself. It's letting them know even if they are going through a difficult time, you are there to support them. Be the biggest cheerleader for the people in your life.

When someone shares a goal or a dream they have with you, say *"Wow!"* instead of immediately asking *"How?"* If it's physically possible, let them know you believe in them and their ability to accomplish their dream. Give them affirmation and encouragement by saying *"Wow!"* There will be plenty of time for asking *"How?"* later.

EMPOWER THEM

When we empower others, we enable them. A form of empowerment is giving someone the resources they need to accomplish something and the freedom to go make it happen.

You can empower your son to clean his room, or you can empower your team members to take on a big project. Both of those situations require you to provide resources. To truly empower them, you must also give them freedom and allow them to take responsibility. Sometimes, empowerment means letting someone try and fail. These opportunities facilitate growth and development.

ENGAGE THEM

One of the definitions for "engagement" found in Merriam-Webster is *"emotional involvement or commitment, or the state of being in gear."* When someone is engaged with something, they are emotionally committed.

You must have influence (leadership) with someone before you can engage them. If you engage them in the right way, you will increase your influence with them. Engage others by helping them discover *why* they should act.

CHAPTER FIFTEEN
BE RELATIONAL

"Relationship capital isn't an asset; it's a privilege."
~ Michael Sciortino

The book that had the most impact on me as a leader while I was working in the corporate world was *The 5 Levels of Leadership* by John C. Maxwell. [1] Although I have always been a reader, I didn't discover leadership books until 2008, and I didn't discover *The 5 Levels* until 2012.

In his book, Maxwell shares what the *5 Levels of Leadership* are and how to climb up the levels to become more effective as a leader. The first level is the *Position Level* where you are given a leadership title or position. However, others only follow you at this level because they "have to." You are the boss. This is the lowest level of leadership (influence).

The second level is the *Permission Level* where you receive permission to lead others. They follow you at this level because they "want to." Maxwell states, *"Level 2 relies on people skills, not power, to get things done. It treats the individuals being led as people, not mere subordinates…If you want to become a better leader, let go of control and start fostering cooperation. Good leaders stop bossing people around and start encouraging them. That is the secret to being a people-oriented leader, because much of leadership is encouragement."*

After learning this, I dramatically changed my leadership style. I realized building relationships with people would significantly increase my influence.

Great leaders are relationship builders. However, in the corporate world, this is (falsely) assumed to be "soft." I think some leaders feel pressured to be "harder" when it comes to leadership. I know I did, especially with the people who worked with me.

To be effective as a leader, you must build strong, solid relationships. As Rick Warren stated, *"You can impress people from a distance, but you must get close to influence them."*

When you get to know someone and build a relationship, they get to know you as well. They will realize you have flaws, strengths, and weaknesses just like everyone else. That's okay. Leaders don't have to be perfect to build trust, but they must be authentic. Admit your flaws and weaknesses and ask others to help you improve them. You will build much more trust and respect when you acknowledge your weaknesses than when you attempt to hide your weaknesses. You don't have to be best friends with everyone who reports to you. In fact, there needs to be a recognition that, as the leader, you sometimes must make tough decisions related to discipline, resources, or promotions. Positive relationships always increase your influence. Leaders should leverage relationships to get results.

RELATIONSHIPS

It may not be a surprise to you, but it was a surprise to me when I first realized people do have different types of personalities. I don't mean people like different kinds of food or have different hobbies. I mean truly realizing different people have preferred styles of communication, preferred ways of interacting with others, and preferred ways of being appreciated, valued, and respected.

A friend gave us a book, *The Five Love Languages,* by Gary Chapman as a wedding gift. Discovering everyone didn't have the same *"love language"* I did was eye opening, not just in my personal relationship with Mack, but also in my professional relationships at work.

When you understand what personality type a person is and what their *"love language"* is, you can better interact with them by focusing on their preferred style instead of yours. I'm not saying fake the relationship, but rather "adjust" your style to match their preferred style. If the person is quiet and reserved, they may not want public recognition for a job well done. They might feel valued with quiet words of praise but feel mortified when publically acknowledged in a large meeting. Take the time to build relationships by consciously identifying the natural preferences of the people around you. Then, make the intentional effort to make deposits of trust into the relationship using their preferred language and style.

RESULTS

Leaders must build relationships to increase their influence, but they must be balanced to achieve results. Balance means having difficult conversations when a team member isn't performing, getting work done, or coming to work on time. It can also mean helping a team member see the job isn't a good fit for them or releasing them to excel elsewhere. Leaders have a job to do and a responsibility to accomplish the mission with and through others. That's why they are chosen to lead. Balancing applies to parenting too. Sometimes, we must make tough choices and say *"no"* when we feel saying *"yes"* wouldn't be in the best interest of our children. They don't want to hear no and may not like us much at the time. But, they will usually end up respecting us for it later. Sometimes, much later.

CHAPTER SIXTEEN
BE UNDERSTANDING

"Never miss a chance to keep your mouth shut."

~ Robert Newton Peck

One of our greatest assets is our ability to understand others through empathic listening. When others feel understood, they are more open to our influence.

However, empathic listening is also one of the most difficult skills to use because truly listening to someone to understand requires our complete attention. There are different levels of listening, and we are all guilty of listening on a very shallow level at times. For example, when a three-year-old child is chatting endlessly about her favorite Disney movie, you may tune out as your mind starts to plan what's next on your agenda.

Frequently, when we are in a conversation, we listen only halfway and focus much of our thinking on what our response will be as soon as there is a chance to jump in and talk. We appear to be politely listening, but in reality, our mind is occupied with something else.

Listening is an incredible way to build your influence with others. Dean Rusk says, *"One of the best ways to persuade others is with your ears - by listening to them."*

Listening, before trying to be heard, is drastically underappreciated in most "leadership" books. It's also drastically underutilized by many "leaders" who are in a formal leadership position and therefore don't believe they need to listen first.

When we listen to someone, they feel valued. When you listen to your team members, children, or even your spouse, you are gaining credibility and influence with them while building a stronger relationship.

To be an understanding leader:

LISTEN TO OTHERS

When we listen deeply to another person, we are listening to the words they say and the words they don't say. We are listening to the feelings they are expressing. We may even reflect the feeling or paraphrase the content to demonstrate understanding. Listening requires our full and complete attention, focused eye contact, and/or the appropriate body language. Once you are sure the other person feels heard and understood and you are sure you understand, then it's okay to respond. Herb Cohen asserts, *"Effective listening requires more than hearing the words transmitted. It demands you find meaning and understanding in what is being said. After all, meanings are not in words but in people."*

Every one of us enjoys the attention from the people we love and those who love us. We crave it. Think of the four year old little boy who wants mom to watch every thing he does. *"Look Mom, watch me!"* he cries out each time he jumps off the tire swing, again and again.

Listening is a great way to demonstrate to anyone that you do care because it requires intentional time and effort. It's a gift you can give to the person you are listening to. They don't have to *wonder* if they are being listened to because they *feel* understood. As Woodrow Wilson explained, *"The ear of the leader must ring with the voices of the people."*

EMPATHIZE WITH OTHERS

Great leaders are great listeners. To successfully influence others at a high level, you must be an effective listener. However, it's not enough to simply ask a question – you must listen to the answer. Dale Carnegie suggested, *"The power of listening is the power to change hearts and minds."* But, you can only do that when you allow yourself to see the perspective of the other person. Empathy is being sensitive to the thoughts and emotions of others without having those thoughts or emotions yourself. It's choosing to step outside of your frame of reference and enter theirs. When you do, you are choosing to look at their situation from their frame of reference. It's a decision to see others as people to be influenced, instead of objects to be moved.

There is a difference between *empathy* and *sympathy*. Empathy is choosing to see something from another's perspective. Sympathy is an inclination to feel the same thing, which isn't always what is needed. Leaders must be able to empathize but don't always need to sympathize.

For example, if a team member asks to be allowed to leave early to attend their son's football game, you can empathize and understand that's important to them. But, if leaving early meant the job wouldn't get done or if it meant not keeping a commitment to a client, then your sympathizing with the team member and allowing them to leave early, when it would hurt the organization, would not be the best option. Other options should be considered.

This happens within our families too. Years ago, my teenage step-son, Eric, had his wisdom teeth removed. Afterward, he wanted to go out with his friends later that night. He said he felt good, and we *empathized* with his desire to go hang out with his friends. But, considering he had just had surgery and was taking pain medication, we didn't *sympathize* with him and didn't let him go.

CHAPTER SEVENTEEN
BE A DEVELOPER

"It is only as we develop others that we permanently succeed."
~ Harvey S. Firestone

Good leaders are always looking for a chance to develop their followers. Great leaders are always looking for a chance to develop more leaders. Questions are the best tool for developing others. Questions develop the thought process, expand the critical thinking skills, and allow you to delegate results, rather than methods.

As a leader, you often have the challenge of delegating to others. The higher up you travel as a formal level leader, the more you will need to delegate. And, how well you delegate determines your effectiveness.

Any task or project carries with it responsibility. How much of that responsibility should you continue to carry when you delegate? As a leader, the more you delegate effectively, the more you will be able to focus your attention on the things only you can do.

If you delegate taking out the trash to your 10 year old son, you may free up time to start cooking dinner sooner. But, if you delegate taking out the trash and provide him with step by step directions on how to remove the bag, tie it up, carry it to the large can outside, and insert the new trash bag every time it needs taking out, you haven't freed up much of your time. More importantly, you haven't helped your son learn to think for himself.

Instead, try this. Delegate only the results – keep the kitchen trash can from overflowing. You must start by delegating the result. Give him the project. Coach him using questions: *What does this mean? What does success look like? What would it take to keep the trash can in the desired state?* This is a stewardship delegation – you are delegating the results and the responsibility for making it happen. If it doesn't get done, ask questions to help him think through what is required: *Why is success important? How can you be sure to do it regularly? What resources do you need from me?*

It takes more time to delegate this way in the short term. Long term, it develops the person at an entirely new level and frees up your time.

Unfortunately, questions are an underutilized tool for many leaders. Great leaders realize questions are a powerful way to connect with and develop others.

Whether you are asking the questions to your team members or your children, questions allow you to empower and engage them. Sam Walton stated, *"Asking and hearing people's opinions has a greater effect on them than telling them, 'Good job.'"*

Asking questions shows respect, allows you to learn how someone is thinking, allows you to see another perspective, and allows them to influence you, which increases your influence with them.

Thought provoking questions facilitate deeper communication. The key is to ask the question in the right way, and often, ask a follow-up question. When you are intentionally working to develop someone, answer a question with a question. It takes longer, but the rewards are huge relative to delegating responsibility, developing, and growing your team.

Ask for recommendations and solutions. Ask how they propose to do something. Ask why or why not. Ask what the barriers are. Ask what the pitfalls might be. Ask what the opportunities are. Ask what else you need to know or consider. And, listen to the answers. If you aren't listening to the answers, there is no point in asking the questions. As Bruce Lee declared, *"A wise man can learn more from a foolish question than a fool can from a wise answer."* Here are some extremely useful questions when delegating results:

How can I help you?

What do you think?

What's the first step? What's the next step?

What could happen? What else might happen?

What is your plan?

What action have you taken so far?

What caused this outcome?

How can you learn more about the project?

What resources are available?

What if that doesn't work, what will you do?

What was the lesson? Who else should know?

What should you do different next time?

What are your roadblocks? What are the options?

What's the overall impact?

What should I know?

Who can help?

CHAPTER EIGHTEEN
BE HUMBLE

"Having the tenacity to lead, and the humility to serve are the key ingredients of Transformative Leadership."

~ Amir Ghannad

If you had the opportunity to meet any great person from the past who was a highly effective and very successful leader, you would find he or she was humble. You may have heard *"Pride goes before a fall."* Angola Prison Warden Burl Cain said it this way, *"You've got to be humble, so you don't stumble."*

Humility is the foundation for leadership and influence. Humility helps you stay centered. Humility comes with maturity. Of course, maturity most often comes from learning lessons the hard way. However, we can also learn from the mistakes of others without repeating them ourselves. To be clear, I'm not saying you shouldn't have pride in a job well done. If you worked hard, accomplished something, or reached a goal, you should have some satisfaction in having done so. Your brain is hardwired to reward you with endorphins when you accomplish a task which will help inspire you to set a new goal or target.

The problem isn't thinking *"I have done well,"* but rather thinking, *"What a great person I am to have done it!"* There's a fine line between confidence and arrogance. It's called humility. Confidence is knowing you can do something. Arrogance is boasting about your abilities. Arrogance is a huge turn off. Remember the words of author and speaker Simon Sinek, *"Great leaders don't need to act tough. Their confidence and humility serve to underscore their toughness."*

As leaders, it's important to be humble because we are always setting the example for those who follow us. Be sure to set the right example for the right reason.

ADMIT MISTAKES

We all make mistakes. If you aren't making mistakes, you aren't doing anything! No one expects their leader to be perfect and never make a mistake. Leaders get into trouble when they try to cover up a mistake. Sooner or later, it will be discovered. The best thing to do when you make a mistake is to own it and take action to correct it. In the words of Thomas Merton, *"Pride makes us artificial and humility makes us real."* Those who are following you already know you aren't perfect. What they want to know is, *"Do you know it?"* Admitting mistakes and acting to correct them will increase your influence. Trying to cover them up will decrease your influence.

RECOGNIZE LIMITATIONS

Guard against having pride by remembering your limitations and weaknesses. Recognize what you can and cannot do, should and should not do, will and will not do. No one is great at everything. If something is not in your strength zone, ask for help rather than causing an issue because you are too proud to seek help.

Author C. S. Lewis said this about pride: *"There is no fault which makes a man more unpopular and no fault which we are more unconscious of in ourselves. And, the more we have it ourselves, the more we dislike it in others."*

GIVE CREDIT

Great leaders know they can't accomplish much without the help of their team and others around them. It's perfectly acceptable to say *"Thank you!"* when accepting a compliment, but don't hesitate to shine the spotlight on those who helped you make it happen.

Rick Pitino stated, *"Humility is the true key to success. Successful people lose their way at times. They often embrace and overindulge from the fruits of success. Humility halts this arrogance and self-indulging trap. Humble people share the credit and the wealth."*

BECOME LESS SELF-CENTERED

It's not that you don't realize your self-worth, but rather you don't focus on it. It's important to remember from your frame of reference the world appears to revolve around you. But for the rest of the world, it doesn't. Becoming more focused on other people and less focused on yourself will increase your influence with everyone you meet.

As Pastor Rick Warren stated, *"True humility is not thinking less of yourself; it's thinking of yourself less. Humility is thinking more of others. Humble people are so focused on serving others, they don't think of themselves."*

BECOME MORE VALUE-CENTERED

The first step in overcoming too much pride are to realize it, acknowledge it, and then work to intentionally embrace humility as a bigger value in your life. If this is a weakness, find a trusted mentor who has a strong foundation of humility and ask them to help you. We all stand taller when standing on the shoulders of someone else.

CHAPTER NINETEEN
BE TEACHABLE

"I don't think much of a man who is not wiser today than he was yesterday."

~ Abraham Lincoln

To be teachable means open to being taught. This definition implies that being teachable is different than simply learning on your own. We are teachable only when we are open to learning from others.

We are teachable when we ask for, listen to, and accept constructive feedback from others. Even when we don't ask for feedback, we should listen to and accept it. In my book, *Straight Talk: The Power of Effective Communication*, I shared this story of a time when I needed to be teachable.

In 2007, I was working in a doctor's office when the office manager was terminated. I was interviewed for the position, selected and I felt they owed it to me. I had more pride than humility, and I wasn't very teachable. I thought I was capable of doing a better job than anyone else. As the leader, I wanted to control everything that went on. I wanted everything to come through me because I thought I was the only one who could and should make decisions in the office.

One morning, we were getting ready to open the office, and one of the older ladies who worked there sat down with me. She said, *"Ria, you are very capable. But, everyone is concerned because you act like you know everything – you don't."*

She was taking a risk by sharing that with me – I was her new boss. She didn't say it specifically, but she was telling me I didn't have humility. I wasn't teachable. I knew in my heart, she was right. Looking back, I am not proud of how I acted in those days. But, I am proud of how I responded to what she said.

It was a defining moment for me. I had a choice to be teachable or not. Instead of getting mad, I actually embraced what she said. It took time, but I changed my behavior and my feelings. More importantly, I learned I didn't know everything after all. In fact, the more I learned, the more I realized what I didn't know. John Wooden said, *"It's what we learn after we know it all that counts."*

Leaders must be open to continuously learning in order to be able to give more to their followers. And, part of that learning is learning to be teachable. Listen to, consider carefully, and if necessary make adjustments based on the feedback you receive from others.

Sometimes, there's feedback you didn't ask for. Sometimes, there's feedback you didn't like to hear. But, anytime we receive feedback, we should accept it. Whether we feel it's warranted or not doesn't matter.

Teachability expands and enlarges your gifts, talents, and abilities.

Here are some ways you can be teachable as a leader:

ASK FOR FEEDBACK FROM FOLLOWERS

Only the most secure leaders will ask for feedback from those they are leading. The first step is making sure the relationship is strong enough to ensure you receive honest feedback. Those you are leading must feel secure enough to give you feedback and trust you won't retaliate against them in some way. It takes a strong leader to be able to create that type of relationship in the first place. Be sure to leverage your relationships and ask for feedback from the right people.

Often, you can do this by asking questions like: *What would you do if you were in my position? How else could I have handled that situation?*

ASK FOR FEEDBACK FROM OTHER LEADERS

Consider your peers as a source to learn from. Napoleon Hill taught about the power of a "Master Mind" in his books. A master mind is a group of two or more people who are focused on a common goal. When that happens, it creates a synergistic relationship where one plus one equals three, 10, or 100. Peer groups or learning from others who are in a similar situation as you can be very valuable – but make sure you are getting feedback from someone who has successfully done what you are trying to do. Don't listen to advice from someone who simply has an opinion – because everyone does.

ASK FOR FEEDBACK FROM A MENTOR

A mentor can provide very valuable feedback. Sometimes, you may have more than one mentor or a mentor for different areas of your life and leadership. If you don't have someone in your life who can mentor you, you can still be teachable by studying the books of someone who has been successful as a leader. By choosing your source for mentorship carefully and applying their advice thoughtfully, you are displaying a teachable spirit. Learn from the mistakes as well as the successes of others. Consider their lessons carefully and ask yourself how you can benefit from it.

CHAPTER TWENTY
BE CURIOUS

"Millions saw the apple fall, but Newton was the only one who asked why."

~ Bernard Baruch

Curiosity isn't a trait of personality – it's a state of mind. Anyone *can* be curious. The successful leader will be a curious leader. Why? Because curiosity is the state of mind that opens your thoughts to new perspectives. Curiosity means you are opening new doors, doing new things, and discovering new ways to move forward.

Samuel Johnson said it best, *"Curiosity is one of the most permanent and certain characteristics of a vigorous intellect."* A high level of curiosity is a sign of a high level of intelligence. Intelligent leaders know they always have a lot to learn, regardless of how much they already know. Leaders should be curious because curiosity:

INCREASES INFLUENCE WITH OTHERS

Harry Lorayne declared, *"Curiosity killed the cat, but where human beings are concerned, the only thing a healthy curiosity can kill is ignorance."*

When you are curious about someone, you are increasing your influence because you are telling them you are willing to learn from and about them. Influence is based on respect and trust. When someone feels you care about them and want to understand them, they will be much more open to your influence because they will respect and trust you. Stephen R. Covey said, *"Seek first to understand, then to be understood."*

Be curious about people. To build influence, seek to understand someone else's viewpoint. Then, they will be more open to understanding yours.

CREATES OPPORTUNITIES

Curiosity leads to creative thinking. Creative thinking leads to creative solutions. In the words of Walt Disney, *"We keep moving forward, opening new doors, and doing new things because we're curious, and curiosity keeps leading us down new paths."*

Be curious about challenges. When you encounter a challenge, ask yourself what makes it challenging and what the options for navigating it are. Ask yourself or others what the positive things about this challenge are and how overcoming it will help you improve. When one door closes, don't spend time wishing it hadn't closed - look for another door to open.

STIMULATES GROWTH

When you are curious about something you are in a growth and learning state. Curiosity is about discovering. Discovering is about growing. As William Arthur Ward said, *"Curiosity is the wick in the candle of learning."*

Curiosity allows you to ask deep questions, probe a situation, and think carefully about the answers. Pay very close attention to what is going on around you. When something happens unexpectedly, make sure you are intentionally seeking the cause and looking for unexpected possibilities that are now available to you.

Be curious about possibilities. It will stimulate your growth and help you stimulate the growth of others. Growth is not comfortable because all growth happens outside of your comfort zone. You must become comfortable with the tension caused by growth and recognize the value created by the tension. A rubber band is useful only when it's being stretched. Likewise, leaders are most useful when they are being stretched due to growth. Growth separates leaders from followers.

SOLVES PROBLEMS

One tiny, three letter word, can solve even very large problems. As the leader, it's your job to ask *"Why?"* Asking *why* something happened or *why* it is the way it is will allow you to get down to the root cause of the issue.

There is a very popular story about the Jefferson Memorial eroding faster than it should have compared to other memorials nearby. Until someone started asking *"Why?,"* the National Park Service couldn't figure out the cause. *Why* was the monument deteriorating faster? Harsh chemicals were used to remove bird droppings. *Why* were the birds there? They were eating bugs. *Why* were the bugs there? They were attracted to the special lighting at a certain time of day. When they changed the lighting schedule and quality, the bugs didn't come around as much. The bird problem, or rather the bird dropping problem, nearly disappeared along with the erosion problem.

Be curious about problems. However, when you ask *why* make sure everyone knows you aren't seeking to blame but merely seeking a cause. That's the difference between asking *"Why?"* and asking *"Who?"* If you ask *"Who did this?"* it implies someone is to blame and puts people on the defensive very quickly. Problem solving will shut down. If you ask *"Why something happened?"* you aren't placing blame, but seeking the cause in order to find the most effective solution.

CHAPTER TWENTY ONE
BE TRUSTWORTHY

"If someone you're trying to influence doesn't trust you, you're not going to get very far; in fact, you might even elicit suspicion because you come across as manipulative."

~ Amy Cuddy

Of all the characteristics of great leaders, being trustworthy is probably worth more than all the rest combined. Actually, all the others help build trust.

It doesn't matter if your vision is great, you are well liked, can communicate well, and listen well. If people don't trust you, they won't follow you.

Merriam-Webster defines trustworthy as *"deserving of faith and confidence."* You can't make someone trust you. Trust must be earned over time. You can earn faith and confidence (trust), but you can't demand it, force it, or require it. You can only earn it by getting all the other leadership characteristics right.

Those who build trust are building their leadership foundation, brick by brick. Every encounter with someone is an opportunity to add another brick to the foundation or wipe away the entire foundation.

Distrust disrupts. In an organization, it creates low moral, decreases productivity, increases turnover, creates havoc with teams, and causes others to question your motives. In a family, it destroys relationships that sometimes have taken years to build.

The level of trust you can create as a leader determines the impact you will have.

The foundation of trust is built on your credibility as a person. You must have a high level of personal credibility and integrity with yourself before you can start to earn credibility with others. Stephen M. R. Covey identified two basic types of trust: *Self-Trust* (confidence in yourself, setting and achieving goals, keeping commitments, walk the talk, etc.) and *Relationship Trust* (faith and confidence placed in you by others).

You can't force trust, you can only earn it. Here are three major behaviors that will help you earn both types of trust:

KEEP COMMITMENTS

Keeping commitments is the first responsibility of a leader when it comes to building trust. It starts with keeping commitments to yourself. You can build your personal integrity by carefully choosing and keeping the commitments you make to yourself. Don't make a commitment you can't keep. If you aren't sure you can do it, don't commit to doing it.

If you don't have a high level of personal credibility, you won't have a high level of interpersonal credibility.

Statistics on broken "New Year's Resolutions" are always interesting because they reflect that a large percentage of the population doesn't have a high level of credibility. They make commitments to themselves about their personal goals and behaviors such as losing weight, quitting smoking, exercising more, and so on. But, the vast majority of them have fallen by the wayside within 30 days. If we won't keep a commitment we made to ourselves, we won't keep commitments we made to others.

TRUST OTHERS

We see the world as we are, not as it is. In other words, our perspective of the world is largely filtered by our frame of reference. If someone is color blind, they believe the world is dull and gray, because that is how they see it. In reality, the world is beautiful with colors that other people *can* see.

If we don't show trust in others, it's because the world is filtered by our frame of reference – that people aren't trustworthy. Therefore, we won't be able to earn the trust of others. As the leader, it's your job to extend trust first.

WALK THE TALK

We respect those who lead by example. Words account for very little of the message we actually convey to someone. What counts more than anything is what we actually do.

If you want someone to listen to you, you must be willing to listen first. If you want others to respect you, you must respect them. If you want others to be honest with you, you must be honest and transparent with them. If you expect loyalty from your followers, you must first be loyal to them. If you want your team to deliver results, you must first equip them. If you want a raise, you must first be responsible.

Oprah Winfrey said this about walking the talk, *"Real integrity is doing the right thing, knowing that nobody's going to know whether you did it or not."*

What counts is what you do, especially when no one is watching, because that reveals your true character.

If you walk the talk at all times, you will create credibility with yourself and with others.

CHAPTER TWENTY TWO
BE SELFLESS

"The high destiny of the individual is to serve rather than to rule."
~ Albert Einstein

Servant leadership is a term coined in the 1970's by Robert Greenleaf. However, the concept has been around since the beginning of influence. A great example: Jesus, King of kings, washed the feet of His disciples.

High level leaders are more naturally inclined to be servant leaders or selfless leaders. Effective leaders recognize the need to put others before themselves. Intuitively, leaders understand going the second mile isn't second rate. It's first class. Most of us already know when we put others first, we get far more than they do. As Douglas Lawson said, *"We exist temporarily through what we take, but we live forever through what we give."*

Low impact leaders often struggle with the concept of "servant leadership" or being selfless in their leadership role. That's because they cannot get past their formal leadership position. They expect everyone else to serve them.

They don't understand true leadership and influence are built on the relationships you have, not the title you hold. You can create a much better relationship with someone when you are willing to think of yourself less, and think of them more. Max DePree put it this way, *"The first responsibility of a leader is to define reality. The last is to say 'Thank you.' In between, the leader is a servant."*

When you accept the responsibilities of being a leader, you accept the responsibility of considering others before yourself. This means thinking of yourself less, and others more, in terms of your leadership. It means being the biggest cheerleader, encourager, and leading by example.

If there is a big project due on a tight deadline, you

can demonstrate selfless leadership by being the first to get to work and the last to leave. Self-less leadership means not slipping out at 4:30pm on Friday when you always expect everyone else to work until 5:00pm. If someone has to work late occasionally, do your part to help *and then some.*

It also means holding yourself to a higher standard than others. If you expect a generous, giving, spirit among your team members, or your children for that matter, you must first be what you expect others to be.

Sometimes, being a selfless leader means getting your hands dirty. I was working as an office manager in a physician office many years ago when a patient fell in our parking lot. He didn't want to tell anyone, so he went into the lobby bathroom and tried to bind up his scrapes. He was on a blood thinner and ended up getting blood on everything in the bathroom: walls, counter, sink, and floor. When he finally stopped the bleeding, he was okay. But, the bathroom was a mess. When a team member came and told me what happened, I donned some gloves and cleaned the bathroom myself. Don't ask your team to do anything you aren't willing to do first.

BOUNDARIES

Setting aside self-serving behaviors will greatly increase your influence and leadership. However, it's important to have appropriate boundaries set. Self-less doesn't mean self-destruct. Sometimes, we give too much of our time, energy, and attention, until we are running on empty.

We cannot give what we don't have, and if we aren't refueling our own "tank," so to speak, we won't be able to keep helping others. That's why it's so important to set your own boundaries for what you can, can't, will, and won't do.

Your boundaries should be based on your values. For example, when I'm speaking at an event, I go above and beyond to add value. Sometimes, that means attending special functions which require me to get up very early or get home very late. Sometimes, it means missing lunch. That's okay – for me that's self-less, putting the needs of others above my own. But, one of my boundaries is that I generally protect my weekends to spend time with Mack. I make very few "work" commitments on weekends because that's a boundary for me. Occasionally, there is a need to be flexible. But for the most part, that's simply a boundary I set and keep unless something extremely urgent comes up. Or, it's something that can't be scheduled for a week day.

Serving others isn't about being their servant. It is simply service-based. It's about leading by serving. Don't hesitate to reach out, be the first to help, remove roadblocks, help someone overcome an obstacle, and help them grow. Your job as the leader is to do the things that cannot be done by anyone else while supporting and equipping those on your team doing everything else.

William Arthur Ward said, *"We must be silent before we can listen. We must listen before we can learn. We must learn before we can prepare. We must prepare before we can serve. We must serve before we can lead."*

Go the second mile to help your team members, and they will go the third mile, fourth mile, and beyond for you in return.

CHAPTER TWENTY THREE
BE TRANSPARENT

"If you have nothing to hide, there is no reason not to be transparent."

~ Mohamed El Baradei

Authenticity is being true to yourself. Transparency is being true with others. Authenticity is "walking the walk" while transparency is "talking the talk." Leaders must do both.

Transparency is a rare and valuable quality in leaders. The unfortunate thing is that our culture today doesn't encourage us to be transparent. We often feel pressure to present an image to the world of having it all together or of perfection, especially in the workplace. We feel pressure to present an image of someone who has all the answers, all the resources, and always has everything under control.

Many people don't realize the value of true transparency and don't feel confident enough in themselves to be transparent.

When we are transparent, we don't hide our flaws. We don't worry about being perfect. Relative to increasing your influence and leadership, it's not about being perfect. It's about being transparent and real.

We all admire the leader who has overcome their flaws, and admits them with humility, far more than we admire the leader who pretends they don't have any.

Being transparent means being the same person in every situation. The wonderful thing about that is how freeing it is. You don't have to worry about acting, saying, or doing something different based on your social situation. You simply are. Socrates said it well, *"May the inner man and the outer be one."*

Transparency doesn't mean you don't respect the opinions of others. It means you don't pretend to agree with them when you don't. For example, I have several friends who are vegan. I respect that. If I go to their home, I take a dish that is vegan, respecting their food values. However, I don't practice a vegan lifestyle in my own home. But, I don't pretend to be vegan while I'm in their home. There is a difference between respecting the values of others and pretending to share them. Respecting values builds influence and trust. Pretending to share values creates distrust.

As Ralph Waldo Emerson stated beautifully, *"What lies behind us and what lies before us are tiny matters compared to what lies within us."*

When you are transparent you will:

INCREASE TRUST AND INFLUENCE

When you are transparent, you are building solid relationships with a high level of trust because people know they can trust you to tell the truth, even if you don't want to or have to. The relationships of a transparent leader are formed on a solid foundation of trust. One of my favorite quotes on transparency is, *"A lack of transparency results in distrust and a deep sense of insecurity."* (Dalai Lama)

Transparency is the purest form of truth telling. As my husband Mack says, *"Transparency is telling the truth when you don't have to simply because you want to."* When you are a transparent leader, you are a highly influential leader because transparency and trust multiply your influence.

As leaders, we are in the position of establishing trust in the relationships with those who follow us. It's critical to establish and maintain trust for effective leadership. Without it, your influence as a leader will be little to none.

We establish trust by demonstrating a high level of

character and integrity. This requires transparency and alignment with what we say and what we do. If you say one thing and do something different, you will quickly lose trust with your followers. In relationships, the little things are the big things.

When you are not transparent you will:

DECREASE TRUST AND INFLUENCE

Stephen M. R. Covey stated, *"Violations of integrity are the most difficult of all to restore in all relationships, whether they are personal, family, professional, organizational, or in the marketplace."*

When we fail to be transparent, we will decrease trust in the relationship and influence with the person.

That doesn't mean trust cannot be restored, over time, but it does means it's not automatically extended to us again and again if we have demonstrated a lack of transparency. Once trust is violated, it takes time, deliberate effort, and energy to work to restore the relationship. It can be done, and sometimes, the relationship will be stronger. But sometimes, trust is also lost forever.

Like everything truly worth having, transparency doesn't cost us anything. It cannot be bought. Howard Schultz said, *"I think the currency of leadership is transparency. You've got to be truthful. I don't think you should be vulnerable every day, but there are moments where you've got to share your soul and conscience with people and show them who you are, and not be afraid of it."*

CHAPTER TWENTY FOUR
BE FORGIVING

"You only have to forgive once. To resent, you have to do it all day, every day."

~ M. L. Stedman

A big part of leadership is developing accountability. However, great leaders balance that with the need to also demonstrate forgiveness. Great leaders focus on moving forward together if that can be done without resentment on either side, and there is value for both parties in doing so. Or apart, if the consequences for whatever happened call for ending the relationship.

Whichever path is chosen, great leaders know forgiveness is required on both sides. If you can't forgive, you can't move forward, together or apart.

Nelson Mandela was an example of a great leader who saw the benefits of forgiveness. He fought for democracy and against apartheid and racism in South Africa. He was arrested and served 27 years in prison for "conspiring against the government." After his release, he later became the president of South Africa. In 1993, he jointly won the Nobel Peace Prize with Frederik Willem de Klerk *"…for their work for the peaceful termination of the apartheid regime, and for laying the foundations for a new democratic South Africa."* [1]

Mandela knew to move forward, there must be forgiveness. He had to forgive being imprisoned for nearly three decades of his life – that's a lot to forgive.

He is one of the greatest examples in history of a leader who was able to forgive and accomplish great things as a result. He is an incredible example of someone who rose above his circumstances with an idea and an ideal he was willing to fight for, live for, and even die for. Mandela knew forgiveness was something required of him both as a person and as a leader. You cannot be very successful as a person or very effective as a leader if you hold on to bitterness, anger, resentment, or hate.

FORGIVENESS AS A PERSON

On the personal side, there are many situations in life where we have the opportunity to forgive. Whether we choose to do so is a very personal decision, but there is no doubt choosing not to forgive will only hurt you.

Lewis Smedes stated, *"To forgive is to set a prisoner free and discover that the prisoner was you."*

The energy required to remain unforgiving is something that will drain you because you have to work to remind yourself to hate someone or resent them, every single day. When you forgive, even if the relationship isn't the same, you let go of the bitterness, anger, resentment, and find freedom for yourself.

I experienced this in my own life. I knew the day I left home at 19, holding on to hate, anger, or bitterness, for even one minute would allow what happened to me to affect the rest of my life. And, I wasn't willing to do that. It's not always easy to forgive. When you feel you have been wronged, you feel you are owed something in return for the hurt and the pain. But, you can and should let it go. We can move forward in spite of it all. It takes a strong person to forgive a wrong done to him. As Mahatma Gandhi said, *"The weak can never forgive. Forgiveness is the attribute of the strong."*

FORGIVENESS AS A LEADER

As a leader, you are responsible for holding others accountable. However, you also must make sure you are giving your team a chance to make mistakes, learn, grow, and "fail forward." We learn far more from our mistakes than our successes. When a team member makes a mistake, you and/or the organization have just paid a price to educate that team member. They are now more valuable (assuming they have learned the lesson and won't repeat the mistake). Give your team room to make mistakes, learn, and grow. They will learn far more from an environment that gives them room to try, learn, try again and succeed. They will also move the company farther much faster. Desmond Tutu said, *"Forgiveness says you are given another chance to make a new beginning."*

There may still be consequences for the mistake. But, enforcing discipline as a leader is very different than issuing punishment. Enforcing discipline isn't pleasant. But when done correctly and based on values, you will earn respect from your team members and increase your influence with those who share the same values.

Issuing punishment because you are mad, upset, lost money, lost a customer, or because the team member simply made a mistake will never increase your influence and grow your leadership.

There are some things you may forgive although you choose to end the relationship. A violation of values (theft, deceit, rudeness to customers or co-workers, etc.) is something you may forgive, but cannot forget. You can still forgive someone as a person without tolerating the behavior among your team. You forgive. You move forward, but you don't move forward together.

CHAPTER TWENTY FIVE
BE FLEXIBLE

"Stay committed to your decisions, but stay flexible in your approach."

~ Tony Robbins

We will often be faced with the need to be flexible. The unexpected will happen, and there will be a need for us to respond by changing something. Anytime change occurs there are challenges and opportunities. Those who are quick to grasp the opportunities will be able to take advantage of them, while those who refuse to be flexible will show up late, if at all, and may miss the opportunity as a result.

Jane Krakowski said, *"You can have a plan, but you have to be flexible. Every day is unpredictable, and you just have to go with the flow."*

When you are flexible, you are first in line for new opportunities. Opportunities to stand out as a leader, opportunities to influence others (including other leaders) around you, opportunities to have input or help make decisions, and opportunities you can't even see yet.

We are all in favor of improvements when they benefit us, but sometimes, we refuse to be flexible if we can't immediately see the benefits.

It's true. Change isn't always for the better. It's also true that if nothing changes, nothing gets better. If everything stays the same, there will be no opportunity for improvement. Leaders don't fight to keep things the same. They fight to improve them.

New technology is a good example. Consider those who refused to buy a car when they first came out. Then, consider how strange that seems today in light of how cars are an integral part of our transportation system.

WHEN WE SHOULD BE FLEXIBLE

I started teaching group fitness many years ago because I enjoy it, and it helps me stay in shape. At the time, the gym manager who hired me was also an instructor and my mentor as I started teaching. She played a huge role in helping me learn to be successful in teaching and set a great example for all of the instructors.

About six months after I started teaching, she resigned. A new manager was hired almost immediately. But, this new manager had different ways of doing things. New policies, new schedules, new everything.

I didn't like it. I didn't want things to change, and I wanted everyone to know it. I wanted the new manager to handle everything just like the one before had. I thought, *"I don't have to be flexible!"*

Looking back now, I'm not proud of my attitude at the time. I could have done so much more to embrace the change and make the new manager feel welcome. Instead, I let my frustrations about the change be known.

It took a while before I realized I was the one with the problem. It was even longer before I realized I had missed a valuable opportunity to grow my influence and build a relationship with the new manager.

Instead of focusing on moving forward, I was dragging my heels and holding myself back. I got exactly what I deserved. The new manager knew I wasn't willing to be flexible. As a result, I was the last person to know about any upcoming or proposed changes. There wasn't any need to seek my feedback or ask for my input on making things better at the gym because I was resistant to any and all changes.

I did eventually learn my lesson. I realized, regardless of my wishes, change was going to occur in life, at work, and at home. I also realized I was missing out by refusing to be flexible. I was only hurting myself by refusing to embrace change. When it comes to change, be flexible.

WHEN WE SHOULDN'T BE FLEXIBLE

As leaders, we are often called to be flexible and respond to the changing situation. However, there are times where we need to stand strong. Situations are flexible. Values aren't. Values, standards, and ethics are non-negotiable. Those are the things you must stand firm on because those are the things your character is made of.

When it comes to leading others, seek to be the type of leader that's as "flexible as water." Water is extremely flexible, but it can also be strong and powerful when channeled in one direction. According to Lao Tzu, *"Nothing is softer or more flexible than water, yet nothing can resist it."* Commitment to your values affects your relationship with yourself as well as your relationship with others. As a leader, you will often be faced with change. If you want to be effective, you must quickly adapt. Remain flexible until there's a legitimate value-based reason to stand firm and rigid.

Without another job lined up and without giving notice, I once resigned from a company and walked away from a good job when I found the values of the company weren't values I could endorse. I didn't need to be working there. To compromise on that for even one day meant compromising my values. And, I wasn't willing to do that.

CHAPTER TWENTY SIX
BE GENEROUS

"Ultimately what shapes the meaning of our lives is not what we have but what we give."

~ Michael Sciortino

Imagine you are working in a large organization and the company decides to open another facility. They need to hire many more people and decide to promote many of their existing employees to management positions in the new location. They need 100 new managers, and 50 current employees are interested and eligible, including you. It's obvious you aren't competing with any of your co-workers for a promotion because there are 100 positions, and there are only 50 people interested.

Best case, all 50 will be promoted. You are guaranteed to be one of them. No one is worried about trying to out shine anyone else, and there is a great spirit of cooperation among everyone. You see your fellow co-workers as fellow travelers on the same journey as you.

Imagine the same scenario, except now there are only two new management positions available. But, there are still 50 current employees interested and eligible, including you. Suddenly, you are competing against each and every one of your co-workers for those coveted two spots. There is a new tension between co-workers. Communication stalls, morale drops, and tempers flare. Everyone is quick to point out each other's mistakes and trying to make their competition seem less competent. The scarcity caused tension. There isn't enough to go around. Two will win. The others will lose.

As leaders, we can choose to have either an abundance mindset or a scarcity mindset.

We see the world as we are, not as it is. If we look at the world as though there is a giant pie, with only a few slices to go around, we will create the scarcity mindset within ourselves. We fear others might get a bigger piece, or there might not be enough for us. The scarcity mindset, according to Stephen R. Covey is the *"zero-sum paradigm of life."* Those who have a scarcity mindset don't want to share anything: resources, opportunities, credit, knowledge, recognition, or power. Those people won't be happy when anyone else is receiving anything because they believe there isn't enough to go around. They are afraid of not getting their share. They often want someone else's share too.

On the other hand, an abundance mindset is the mindset of a very successful and highly effective leader. These leaders have a deep sense of personal security, confidence, and understand there is enough of everything to go around. They know when they give something away, the return is always greater than what they gave. They choose to be intentionally generous because they know there is enough of everything for everyone.

John C. Maxwell said this about an abundant mindset, *"Leaders who allow a scarcity mindset to work its way into their culture pay a high price. When resources (money, opportunity, recognition) are perceived to be limited, paranoia, fear and politics thrive. In this environment, people become nervous and afraid to make a mistake. As a result, teamwork and innovation suffer. Effective leaders, on the other hand, develop and model an abundance mindset."*

Generous leadership will increase your influence with your team. It will increase your satisfaction as a leader. It will increase your sense of peace within your family.

GIVE OPPORTUNITIES AND EXPERIENCES

Look for opportunities to help others develop.

Whether it's being an "experiential leader" or an "experiential parent," opportunities and experiences are a great way to be generous and help develop others. Instead of attending that regional conference yourself, send one of your team members and ask them to be prepared to give a report to you and the other team members when they return. They will get far more out of it. You will free up your time, build trust, and increase your influence.

GIVE KNOWLEDGE AND RESOURCES

In the spirit of *"teaching someone to fish,"* instead of giving them fish, make sure you are passing on knowledge. Sharing knowledge about everything from your best grilling secrets to how to handle that new software program at work will set you up as the leader who is indispensable because you are always helping and developing others.

Mentorship is one of the best ways to be generous as a leader. Your time is your most valuable resource. Invest it wisely by mentoring others.

GIVE APPRECATION AND CREDIT

You will never say *"Thank you!"* too often. Make sure you are giving credit when earned, recognition when due, and appreciation *always*. It costs nothing and will always increase your influence with others.

CHAPTER TWENTY SEVEN
BE EXCELLENT

"We are what we repeatedly do. Excellence, then, is not an act, but a habit."

~ Aristotle

Excellence is excelling, being the very best, exhibiting greatness, high quality, or something above and beyond the accepted standard. As leaders, we are called to be excellent because we are the example others will follow. What we do becomes who we are. If we settle for mediocre in anything, it becomes a habit.

I was a new employee when my manager gave me a project. She asked me to create an Excel spreadsheet of our department projects and current status. She sent me the assignment via email. I rushed through it throwing together a quick spreadsheet without even formatting it. I sent it back to her within an hour. I thought she would be impressed because I accomplished it so quickly. Within minutes, she sent me a response; *"This is a good start – now work on making it look professional."* Professional? Hmmmm…I had to think about that one. I knew how to format in Excel. At the time, I thought that was not the point of a spreadsheet, and it would take too long to make it neat and professional looking. Bosses want speed more than anything – or so I thought. I worked on it a little more, added a few things like some colored fields and borders around my tables, and sent it back just before noon. I hit send. Satisfied with myself, I went to lunch.

When I got back from lunch, I had another email from her. *"Let's talk."* Uh-oh. That probably wasn't the *"job well done talk"* that I was hoping for.

Later on that afternoon, she asked me to stay and talk to her after others had left for the day. I had no idea what was wrong, but I knew something wasn't going my way. She handed me a print out of the Excel spreadsheet and asked how it looked like to me. I had no idea what the right answer was.

With great kindness (and patience), she showed me the typos and the misspelled words I had completely overlooked in my rush to get the project done. She talked about how important it was to make sure my work reflected high quality. I will never forget what she said, *"Once you put your name on something like this, it's done. For years and years to come, someone will be looking at this, and it will have your name on it. What they see will determine what they think about you and your work ethic."*

She taught me a valuable lesson about excellence. There are times of course, when speed is a factor, but always strive for excellence in everything you do. Establish your reputation as someone who is excellent in all that you do – or don't do it. Giving an extra "inch" will take you an extra mile.

As the leader, it's your job to be excellent while expecting the same from others. Set the standard high for everyone and even higher for yourself. Your team and even your children will rarely, if ever, give more than you do. Be the leader you wish you had.

When you set a high standard of excellence, you raise the bar for yourself, your team, and even your customers. Raising the bar increases your influence – people are attracted to and follow those who are exceptional. No one gets excited about mediocre people or mediocre leaders. Be more.

GIVE THE EXTRA INCH

I saw Rorke Denver, former Navy Seal, speak at a Leadercast event several years ago. He said to everyone in the audience, *"Raise both hands up as high as you can."*

Instantly, everyone stuck both hands high up in the air. Then, he said, *"Raise them one inch higher."* Everyone was able to reach a little higher. Then, he said, *"Please give me just one inch more."* Nearly everyone sat up a little straighter and had one more inch to give.

His point was that most of us often hold something back. We hold a *"reserve."* After we do as much as we think we can, we often realize we can still do more. We can and should learn to tap into that capacity without being asked. Doing so will help you establish excellence in everything you do. Take the time to showcase, polish, proofread, and spell check every area of your life, not just on the spreadsheets. Often, the little details are what will take you from mediocre to excellent and from average to exceptional.

GO THE EXTRA MILE

Look for ways to be excellent as a leader by going above and beyond to connect to your team members. Learn what they like, how they like to be rewarded, what they dream about, and what they dislike. Make them feel like they matter, and you will matter to them.

Look for ways to be excellent as a spouse, friend, or co-worker. Go out of your way to make someone's day special. Drop off some sweets, send a card, or take the time to listen to them. Look for ways to deliver excellent customer service. When you over deliver the unexpected, you will find your credibility with others and your referrals by others increase dramatically.

Many companies, people, and leaders settle for being average and dull. When you are excellent, you will shine.

CHAPTER TWENTY EIGHT
BE PERSEVERANT

"God gives talent. Work transforms talent into genius."
~Anna Pavlova

Perseverance is one of the less glamorous characteristics of successful leaders. We seldom think of the perseverance required to become very effective and highly successful because we often only see the end product or result – the accomplishment.

We often see the result of an athlete's training when they win a gold medal, but we seldom see the sacrifices required to make it happen. Endless hours of training, dedication, study, practice, and hard work occurred behind the scenes before the medal is won.

Most often, it takes 10, 20, or 30 years to become an "overnight success." The road to success is often long, difficult, and uphill the entire way. Perseverance is the characteristic that will launch you above and beyond the masses because it will allow you to keep going long after others have given up.

Famous people who persevered in spite of perceived "failures" include Albert Einstein, Oprah Winfrey, Thomas Edison, Marilyn Monroe, Walt Disney, Stephen King, Michael Jordan, and many others. One thing all of these people have in common is they persevered long after others in similar situations would have quit. That's what allowed them to achieve their goals and dreams.

Everyone will struggle at some point. What we become during the struggle is far more important than what we are struggling to achieve.

As Booker T. Washington stated, *"I have learned that success is to be measured not so much by the position that one has reached in life as by the obstacles which one has overcome while trying to succeed."*

To be perseverant, the goal must be worth working

for. The greater the goal, the greater the sacrifice will be to achieve it. Don't be afraid to dream big and aspire to great things as a leader. But, don't neglect to account for the cost. Aspiring to greatness is easy, achieving it isn't.

Odds are, it will be more difficult, take longer, and cost much more than you think it will. But, it *will* be worth it. Leaders must be perseverant to inspire others to follow them. If you aren't willing to work hard for your goal, dream, or destiny, no one else will either.

To be perseverant, leaders need to be:

DILIGENT

Diligence is steady and constant. Diligent leaders move forward each and every day. They focus on steady progress, an inch at a time if necessary. They know constant progress will add up over time.

Diligent leaders know success may be just around the corner. But if you give up, you will never achieve it. As Thomas Edison said, *"Many of life's failures are men who did not realize how close they were to success when they gave up."*

Diligent leaders aren't afraid to try a new tactic or a new strategy. If it doesn't work, they can and will always try something else. They will note the lesson and move on. Dr. Henry Cloud suggested, *"If you have already been trying hard, maybe trying harder is not the way. Try different."*

DEDICATED

Dedicated leaders find energy in their commitment to their purpose. They are willing to work for their cause, and they are dedicated to leading others to follow them in pursuit of it. Few ever follow an uncommitted leader for very long. Most people won't follow them at all.

Dedicated leaders know failures are only failures if they quit and give up. Henry Ford had a good perspective on failure. He said, *"Failure is the opportunity to begin again more intelligently."*

Failures, when perceived as opportunities, are often the catalyst to progress. Dedicated leaders don't let roadblocks stop them. They simply find another way to get to where they want to be. According to Elbert Hubbard, *"The line between failure and success is so fine that we…are often on the line and do not know it."*

DETERMINED

Determined leaders refuse to quit. They know it might be a long, difficult journey, but they also know they only have to take one step at a time. They know determination creates motivation and momentum. They refuse to make excuses because they believe as George Washington Carver believed, *"Ninety-nine percent of failures come from people who have the habit of making excuses."*

Turning around isn't an option for a determined leader. They simply look for another door to open when one door closes. Determined leaders can relate to these words from Napoleon Hill, *"Every successful person finds that great success lies just beyond the point when they're convinced their idea is not going to work."*

CHAPTER TWENTY NINE
BE GRATEFUL

"Gratitude can transform common days into thanksgivings, turn routine jobs into joy, and change ordinary opportunities into blessings."

~ William Arthur Ward

Gratitude is the feeling of being thankful. It's joy, appreciation, or being grateful for something or someone. When you have gratitude, it's impossible to hold bitterness in your heart.

The benefits of practicing gratitude are proven scientifically. While I was researching and writing *"Fearfully and Wonderfully Made: A Grateful Heart"* I was astounded by all the studies that show how gratitude helps you: live longer, decrease stress, become more resilient, become less self-centered, become kinder, be healthier, sleep better, increase productivity, better achieve goals, become less materialistic, become more optimistic, become more spiritual, and have better self-esteem. It sounds like an ad for a wonder drug. And yet, you don't need a prescription to get it. It costs nothing, and it's available to all of us. To obtain all those benefits, we need only practice being grateful for our blessings.

Above and beyond everything practicing gratitude does for us personally, it makes an incredible difference in our relationships. *Every* relationship in your life, at home, at work, at school, at church, and anywhere else will improve when you express gratitude to the people you encounter along the way. Ralph Marston said, *"Make it a habit to tell people thank you. To express your appreciation, sincerely and without the expectation of anything in return. Truly appreciate those around you, and you'll soon find many others around you."*

Gratitude makes people feel appreciated, valued, and respected. When people feel you appreciate, value, and respect them, you are increasing your influence with them. Remember, every encounter you have with someone is an opportunity to build trust and increase influence or to create distrust and decrease influence. Relationships with others are based on an "emotional bank account." Every encounter either adds an *emotional deposit* into the account (building trust), or takes an *emotional withdrawal* out of the account (creating distrust).

Very successful and highly effective leaders won't accomplish much alone. We all have people in our lives who help us, encourage us, and support us. When you practice gratitude in your relationship with someone, you put a small deposit into the relationship account. *"Thank you!"* is probably the most powerful phrase in any language. I don't think it's possible to over appreciate someone and what they do for you. No one gets tired of feeling genuinely appreciated. When we feel appreciated for what we do, we feel inclined to do more. Thus, we can intentionally create a beautiful cycle of kindness and appreciation in any relationship.

In their book, *A Carrot A Day: A Daily Dose of Recognition for Your Employees*, Adrian Gostick and Chester Elton stated very clearly, *"Great managers (leaders) praise effort. Reward Results…A daily dose of appreciation creates a stronger workplace where people come, stay, and are committed to your goals."*

Showing appreciation for your team members and co-workers will increase your influence with them. But, it's just as important, perhaps more so, to express appreciation and practice gratitude in your personal relationships because those are the ones where we are most likely to become "overdrawn."

For some reason, the people we love the most are the ones who often see us at our worst. We are more likely to take them for granted or to drift into a habit of not expressly demonstrating appreciation for the "little" things. "Little" things (both deposits and withdrawals) can become "big" things in relationships over time. Because we are making withdrawals, sometimes without even being aware of it, we must be very intentional and consistent about making deposits.

Here are some ways to practice gratitude:

> Make a list of people in your life you are grateful to, and for, past and present. Choose one (or more). Call them, write them a note, send an email, or have a good old-fashioned visit and tell them you are grateful for them and why. What are some of the "little things" you have taken for granted in the past?

> What do you love and appreciate about your children, spouse, or parents? What are you grateful for in regard to your friends or loved ones? What do you value about them? Think for a few minutes about the good characteristics of the loved ones in your life. Then, share with them today how you are grateful for them and how they impact you.

> Make a few notes here on how you can and should express appreciation for the "little" things.

CHAPTER THIRTY
BE THOUGHTFUL

"The very essence of leadership is that you have to have vision. You can't blow an uncertain trumpet."

~ Theodore Hesburgh

The vast majority of leaders today don't spend enough time thinking. You should have dedicated thinking time built into your schedule. Few leaders do. There is always pressure to be doing something and dedicated thinking time doesn't feel like it's actually accomplishing anything. As S. I. Parker said, *"Thought is important because it is thought that generally precedes action."*

It's important to remember activity doesn't necessarily equal accomplishment. Focused activity can help you accomplish great things, while activity alone is simply busy work. If your wheels are spinning but you aren't moving forward, you are stuck. Leaders must be thoughtful in order to maximize the opportunities of today by remembering the lessons of the past and considering the possibilities in the future. When we are leading others, we carry the responsibility of making sure we are going in the right direction.

Where you do your intentional thinking is an important consideration. Get outside if possible. Walk in the woods, a park, go for a jog, or sit in your quiet space. Try to eliminate distractions as much as possible. Turn off your phone, or better yet, leave it elsewhere. Make sure you have a way to capture your thoughts. If you spend time thinking, you want it to be productive. Be sure you have a way to capture the ideas and thoughts you generate.

REFLECTIVE THINKING

Reflective thinking is all about considering the

lessons from the past. Look back and consider what you did or didn't do, why you did or didn't do it, and what you could have and should have done differently. It's not a bad idea to spend a few minutes in reflective thought at the end of every day, but also make sure you are taking some time to reflect on longer spans of time as well.

I like to spend time in reflective thinking about once every three months. A year feels too long – too much time has passed. But, every quarter is enough time to have internalized the lessons and soon enough to make sure the next three months are on course. As the seasons change around me, so do the seasons of life.

Look back at your calendar – did you invest your time well? Look back at your checkbook – did you steward your money well? Look back at your life – did you lead yourself well? Look back at your relationships – did you lead others well?

OPPORTUNITY THINKING

What thoughts are you intentionally thinking about today? Are you reflecting on the realities and opportunities of today? What's interesting about our mind is that, much like a computer, you get out what you put into it. In other words, if you are putting good thoughts about opportunities in today, you will get good thoughts and ideas back out.

James Allen said, *"Our mind may be likened to a garden, which may be intelligently cultivated or allowed to run wild; but whether cultivated or neglected, it must, and will, bring forth. If no useful seeds are put into it, then an abundance of useless weed-seeds will fall therein, and will continue to produce their kind."*

You will encounter opportunities where it's best to say *"no."* But, if you aren't stopping to think about them carefully, you risk saying *"yes"* to the wrong opportunities.

One thing I coach my clients to do is take a blank sheet of paper and write down any and all of their current opportunities. If it's an opportunity that will help them reach their personal definition of success, I ask them to put a circle around it. If it's not, I tell them to cross it out. It doesn't mean that's a bad thing to do – it might be a hobby, something fun with family, or volunteering at church. It does mean it's not an opportunity that will move them in the right direction. If they say *"yes"* to it, they must understand it will take time and energy away from the things that will move them in the right direction. In other words, saying *"yes"* to the *"no"* things will slow you down and hold you back.

STRATEGIC THINKING

Strategic thinking is where you make sure you are considering the vision of your preferred future and making sure you are on course. When it comes to course corrections, the sooner you do it, the better.

This is where you step back and consider the big picture, not just the day-to-day routines. You may not be where you want to be, but you are exactly where you are supposed to be based on the choices you have made leading up to this very moment.

The choices you made yesterday define you today. The choices you make today will define who you become tomorrow.

You're a "gem." Shine bright!

ACKNOWLEDGEMENTS

I don't believe any of us can travel this life journey successfully alone. I would like to thank God for the amazing people He has put in my life! I can't possibly list them all!

I'd like to thank my husband, Mack, for the feedback, synergy, ideas, proof-reading, editing, support, and for being my biggest cheerleader. I love doing life with you!

And, I'd like to thank my readers for being dedicated to personal growth and making a difference in the lives of others.

REFERENCES

Chapter Two:
1) Stephen R. Covey, *The 7 Habits of Highly Effective People* (Free Press, A Division of Simon & Schuster, 1989)

Chapter Three:
1) Rudolph W. Giuliani, *Leadership* (Hyperion, 2002)

Chapter Five:
1) Rick Warren, *The Purpose Driven Life* (Zondervan, 2002)

Chapter Six:
1) Robert Leahy, *The Worry Cure* (Three Rivers Press, a division of Random House, Inc. New York, 2005)

Chapter Ten:
1) Gabrielle Douglas, *Grace, Gold, and Glory: My Leap of Faith* (Zondervan, 2012)

Chapter Thirteen:
1) Simon Sinek, *Start With Why* (Portfolio Penguin, a member of Penguin Group, Inc. 2009)

Chapter Fifteen:
1) John C. Maxwell, *The 5 Levels of Leadership* (Hatchette Book Group, Inc., 2011)

Chapter Twenty Four:
1) Nobel Prize,

http://www.nobelprize.org/nobel_prizes/lists/year/?year=1993 (*Retrieved March 1, 2017*)

Chapter Twenty Nine:

1) Adrian Gostick and Chester Elton, *A Carrot a Day: A daily dose of RECOGNITION for your employees,* (Gibbs Smith Publisher, 2004)

ABOUT THE AUTHOR

Like many, Ria faced adversity in life. Raised on an isolated farm in Alabama, she was sexually abused by her father from age 12 – 19. Desperate to escape, she left home at 19 without a job, a car, or even a high school diploma. Ria learned to be resilient, not only surviving, but thriving. She worked her way through college, earning her MBA with a cumulative 4.0 GPA, and had a successful career in the corporate world of administrative healthcare.

Ria's background includes more than 10 years in administrative healthcare with several years in management including Director of Compliance and Regulatory Affairs for a large healthcare organization. Ria's responsibilities included oversight of thousands of organizational policies, organizational compliance with all State and Federal regulations, and responsibility for several million dollars in Medicare appeals.

Today, Ria is a motivational leadership speaker and author of 11 books. Ria was selected three times to speak on stage at International John Maxwell Certification Events. Motivational speaker Les Brown also invited Ria to share the stage with him in Los Angeles, CA. Ria and her husband, Mack Story, co-founded Top Story Leadership which offers motivational speaking, leadership training, coaching, and consulting.

READ MORE BOOKS BY RIA

The Effective Leadership Series books are written to develop and enhance your leadership skills while also helping you increase your abilities in areas like communication and relationships, time management, planning and execution, and leading and implementing change. Look for more books in the Effective Leadership Series:

- *Straight Talk: The Power of Effective Communication*
- *Change Happens: Leading Yourself and Others through Change*
- *PRIME Time: The Power of Effective Planning*
- *Leadership Gems for Women: 30 Characteristics of Very Successful Women*

READ MORE BOOKS BY RIA

You have hopes, dreams, and goals you want to achieve. You have aspirations of leaving a legacy of significance. You have untapped potential waiting to be unleashed. But, unfortunately, how to maximize your potential isn't something addressed in job or skills training. And sadly, how to achieve success and find significance in life isn't something taught in school, college, or by most parents.

In *ACHIEVE: Maximize Your Potential with 7 Keys to Unlock Success and Significance*, Ria shares lessons to help you become more influential, more successful and maximize your potential in life. Three-page chapters are short, yet powerful, and provide principles on realizing your potential with actionable takeaways. These brief vignettes provide humorous, touching, or sad lessons straight from the heart that you can immediately apply to your own

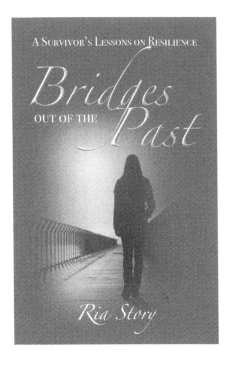

It's not what happens to you in life. It's who you become because of it. We all experience pain, grief, and loss in life. Resilience is the difference between *"I didn't die,"* and *"I learned to live again."* In this captivating book on resilience, Ria walks you through her own horrific story of more than seven years of sexual abuse by her father. She then shares how she learned not only to survive, but also to thrive in spite of her past. Learn how to overcome challenges, obstacles, and adversity in your own life by building a bridge out of the past and into the future.

(Watch 7 minutes of her story at RiaStory.com/TEDx)

READ MORE BOOKS BY RIA

Women are naturally high impact leaders because they are relationship oriented. However, it's a *"man's world"* out there and natural ability isn't enough to help you be successful as a leader. You must be intentional.

Ria packed Leadership Gems for Women with 30 leadership gems which very successful women internalize and apply. Ria has combined her years of experience in leadership roles of different organizations along with years of studying, teaching, training, and speaking on leadership to give you these 30, short and simple, yet powerful and profound, lessons to help you become very successful, regardless of whether you are in a formal leadership position or not.

READ MORE BOOKS BY RIA

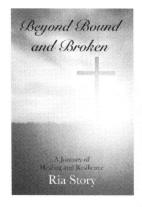

Ria Story

In *Beyond Bound and Broken*, Ria shares how she overcame shame, fear, and doubt stemming from years of being sexually abused by her father. Forced to play the role of a wife and even shared with other men due to her father's perversions, Ria left home at 19 without a job, a car, or even a high-school diploma. This book contains lessons on resilience and overcoming adversity that you can apply in your own life.

In *Ria's Story From Ashes To Beauty*, Ria tells her story of growing up as a victim of sexual abuse from age 12 – 19, and leaving home to escape. She shares how she went on to thrive and learn to help others by sharing her story.

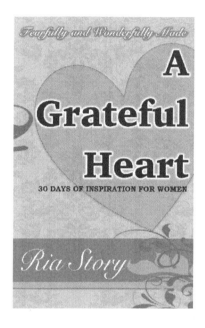

Become inspired by this 30-day collection of daily devotions for women, where you will find practical advice on intentionally living with a grateful heart, inspirational quotes, short journaling opportunities, and scripture from God's Word on practicing gratitude.

READ BOOKS BY MACK STORY

Blue-Collar Leadership and *Blue-Collar Leadership and Supervision* are written specifically for those on the front lines of the Blue-Collar workforce and those who lead them. With 30 short, easy to read chapters, the *Blue-Collar Leadership Series* books contain powerful leadership lessons in a simple and easy to understand format.

Visit www.BlueCollarLeaders.com to learn more, get your free download of the first five chapters from both books, and watch Mack's video related video series.

READ BOOKS BY MACK STORY

It's easier to compete when you're attracting great people instead of searching for good people.

Blue-Collar Leadership® & Culture will help you understand why culture is the key to becoming a sought after employer of choice within your industry and in your area of operation.

You'll also discover how to leverage the components of The Transformation Equation to create a culture that will support, attract, and retain high performance team members.

Blue-Collar Leadership® & Culture is intended to serve as a tool, a guide, and a transformational road map for leaders who want to create a high impact culture that will become their greatest competitive advantage.

READ BOOKS BY MACK STORY

The biggest challenge in process improvement and cultural transformation isn't identifying the problems. It's execution: implementing and sustaining the solutions.

Blue-Collar Kaizen is a resource for anyone in any position who is, or will be, leading a team through process improvement and change. Learn to engage, empower, and encourage your team for long term buy-in and sustained gains.

Mack Story has over 11,000 hours experience leading hundreds of leaders and thousands of their cross-functional kaizen team members through process improvement, organizational change, and cultural transformation. He shares lessons learned from his experience and many years of studying, teaching, and

READ BOOKS BY MACK STORY

Are you ready to play at the next level and beyond?

In today's high stakes game of business, the players on the team are the competitive advantage for any organization. But, only if they are on the field instead of on the bench.

The competitive advantage for every individual is developing 360° of influence regardless of position, title, or rank.

Blue-Collar Leadership® & Teamwork provides a simple, yet powerful and unique, resource for individuals who want to increase their influence and make a high impact. It's also a resource and tool for leaders, teams, and organizations, who are ready to Engage the Front Line to Improve the Bottom Line.

READ BOOKS BY MACK STORY

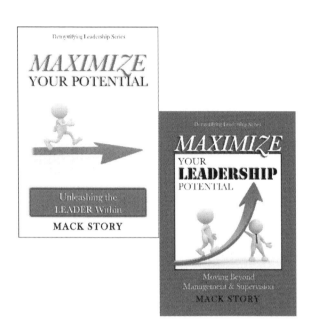

Mack's *MAXIMIXE Your Potential* and *MAXIMIZE Your Leadership Potential* books are the white-collar version of the *Blue-Collar Leadership Series*. These books are written specifically for those working on the front lines and those who lead them. With 30 short, easy to read chapters, they contain powerful leadership lessons in a simple and easy to understand format.

Are you looking for transformation in your life? Do you want better results? Do you want stronger relationships?

In *Defining Influence*, Mack breaks down many of the principles that will allow anyone at any level to methodically and intentionally increase their positive influence.

Mack blends his personal growth journey with lessons on the principles he learned along the way. He's not telling you what he learned after years of research, but rather what he learned from years of application and transformation. Everything rises and falls on influence.

READ BOOKS BY MACK STORY

It's no longer "Buyer Beware!" It's "Seller Beware!" Why? Today, the buyer has the advantage over the seller. Most often, they are holding it in their hand. It's a smart phone. They can learn everything about your product before they meet you. The major advantage you do still have is: YOU!

This book is filled with 30 short chapters providing unique insights that will give you the advantage, not over the buyer, but over your competition: those who are selling what you're selling. It will help you sell yourself.

READ BOOKS BY MACK STORY

10 Foundational Elements of Intentional Transformation serves as a source of motivation and inspiration to help you climb your way to the next level and beyond as you learn to intentionally create a better future for yourself. The pages will ENCOURAGE, ENGAGE, and EMPOWER you as you become more focused and intentional about moving from where you are to where you want to be.

All of us are somewhere, but most of us want to be somewhere else. However, we don't always know how to get there. You will learn how to intentionally move forward as you learn to navigate the 10 foundational layers of transformation.

READ BOOKS BY MACK STORY

High impact leaders align their habits with key values in order to maximize their influence. High impact leaders intentionally grow and develop themselves in an effort to more effectively grow and develop others.

These *10 Values* are commonly understood. However, they are not always commonly practiced. These *10 Values* will help you build trust and accelerate relationship building. Those mastering these *10 Values* will be able to lead with speed as they develop 360° of influence from wherever they are.

Top Story Leadership

Top Story Leadership simplifies foundational leadership principles into everyday language and easy to apply and understand concepts, so organizations and individuals can turn potential into reality. Mack and Ria Story are Certified Speakers and Trainers. They are published authors with more than 20 books available on leadership development, personal growth, and inspirational topics.

- Equip Organizational Leaders
- Encourage Positive Change
- Educate & Empower
- Engage the Front Line to Improve the Bottom Line

LEADERSHIP **Call Us Today!**

334.332.3526

info@TopStoryLeadership.com

TopStoryLeadership.com

Leadership Speaking & Development
Leadership Made Simple

- Leadership Development/Personal Growth
- Organizational Change/Transformation
- Communication/Trust/Relationships
- Time Management/Planning/Execution

What clients have to say…

"My first words are, GET SIGNED UP! This training is not, and I stress, not your everyday leadership seminar! I have attended dozens and sent hundreds to the so-called 'Leadership-Training.' I can tell you that while all of the courses, classes, webinars, and seminars, had good intentions, nothing can touch what Mack and Ria Story provide. I just wish I had it 20 years ago!"
~ Sam McLamb, VP & COO, CMP

"We would highly recommend Mack and Ria as speakers…their presentation was inspirational, thought-provoking, and filled with humor. They taught us some foundational leadership principles."
~ Stephen, President-elect, WCR

"Mack and Ria understand people! The dynamic team made such an impact on our front line supervision that they were begging for more training! We highly recommend Mack and Ria!"
~ Rebecca, Director of Process Improvement, GKN

141

71470600R00085

Made in the USA
Columbia, SC
26 August 2019